ID787755

ALMOST AT THE END

ALMOST AT THE ■ END ■

YEVGENY YEVTUSHENKO

FOREWORD BY
HARRISON E. SALISBURY

TRANSLATED FROM THE RUSSIAN BY
**ANTONINA W. BOUIS, ALBERT C. TODD,
AND YEVGENY YEVTUSHENKO**

HENRY HOLT AND COMPANY   NEW YORK

Published by Henry Holt and Company, Inc.,
521 Fifth Avenue, New York, New York 10175.
Distributed in Canada by Fitzhenry & Whiteside,
195 Allstate Parkway, Markham, Ontario L3R 4T8.

Library of Congress Cataloging in Publication Data
Yevtushenko, Yevgeny Aleksandrovich, 1933–
Almost at the end.
1. Yevtushenko, Yevgeny Aleksandrovich, 1933–
Translations, English.   I. Bouis, Antonina W.
II. Todd, Albert.   III. Title.
PG3476.E96A217   1987   891.71'44   86-22800
ISBN 0-8050-0148-4
First Edition
Designed by Susan Hood
Printed in the United States of America
1 3 5 7 9 10 8 6 4 2

ISBN 0-8050-0148-4

C O N T E N T S

F O R E W O R D

BY HARRISON E. SALISBURY

There are three fat folders in one of my files with the name Yevtushenko on them. They are wedged between a folder marked E. B. White and another marked Andrei Voznesensky. The folders are jammed with information about Yevtushenko—articles, letters, my own observations. Everything is there but Yevtushenko himself and there is no possible way in which this man can be put in a file or captured on paper.

I have known Zhenya since 1959 when everything was bubbling in Khrushchev's Russia and he and Voznesensky and Belle Akhmadulina recited their poetry to crowds of 10,000 or 20,000 or more in Mayakovsky Square, a sight never seen before—or since.

Since those days there is hardly a spot on earth that Yevtushenko has not penetrated, proclaiming his verse in the dramatic style of traditional Russian poetry recitals, stirring up storms almost everywhere he traveled just as he has done for more than a quarter century in his own country. He tells us in *Almost at the End* that as a child he was fearful of physical pain. If that was ever true he has demonstrated in a tumultuous life a willingness to take bold risks both at home and abroad such as few if any of his poet peers have undergone.

There has always been confusion, particularly abroad, about Yevtushenko the poet and Yevtushenko the political advocate. And, when we read Yevtushenko's latest volume, the reason for this confusion becomes readily apparent: Yevtushenko is a man who has strong beliefs about everything—everything in his own country, everything he sees around the world, and the passion flows like blood in his veins into the words he uses and the subjects that attract him. He has never been neutral since his days as a waif along the Transsiberian tracks in World War II.

If to some Yevtushenko has seemed more political than is expected of a poet, perhaps the fault lies with expectation rather than with tradition. Poets have always taken sides and this has been true of American poets from early days down through Longfellow, Whitman, and into the time of Robert Lowell. No one has ever been in doubt as to the political views of Robert Penn Warren, and the mid-nineteenth-century poets of England were on the front line for such causes as liberty in Italy and Greece. And, to be certain, Russia's great poets spoke out against the evils of Czarism and later raised their voices for Revolution.

To me Yevtushenko is a poet in the great and brave tradition of Russian letters. He was the first and still is the most outspoken against Stalin and the dangers of a revival of Stalinism. He was the first and remains the most outspoken against Babi Yar and anti-Semitism. He spoke out against the censors and against shackles on Russian writers in the days before their cause became a chorus of protest from abroad.

Yevtushenko publicly rebuked Nikita Khrushchev for his slanderous outburst against the sculptor Ernst Neizvestny and others of the young Soviet artistic generation. A few days before his death Khrushchev called Yevtushenko to his bedside and apologized.

Now Yevtushenko and his ally Andrei Voznesensky are leading a drive to persuade the Gorbachev regime to grant writers greater creative freedom, to publish the great suppressed master works such as Pasternak's *Doctor Zhivago* and the poems of Akhmatova and Mandelshtam.

It is true that Yevtushenko's politics are not without fault—whose are? In a difficult world he has been found most of the time in the camp of the right cause.

Nor should it be said that his writing is without flaws. In part, our perception is influenced by the difficulty of translation. He is a pure Russian poet and his idiom rings true as steel in the subzero Siberian winter. It is a difficult form to convey in another language. Often his verse is blunt and challenging. But the poetic chord is there. American taste has come to favor the more allusive, the more obscure, the mystic, sometimes the unintelligible. Yevtushenko is always intelligible. He is free in his poetic allusions but we can always understand what he is saying without a second reading. There is more of Whitman in his nature than of Pound. Much more.

Now in *Almost at the End* Yevtushenko has embarked on a creative experiment—the combination of prose and poetry in what seems to me to be a new, attractive and enormously effective form. It gives strength and body to his poetics and it lends emotion and color to his prose. Here is an outrush of feeling as tumultuous as anything Yevtushenko has ever written. The words, the images, the cries of anguish and exaltation pour forth like a torrent from the Lena in the quick Russian *rasputitsa*, the thaw of the short spring.

In presenting us with cinematographic insights into his life, his travels (particularly into the harsh dictatorial states of Latin America), flashes from his childhood, Yevtushenko invests his work with an extraordinary excitement, an unrestrained force.

Philosophically, this work marks a powerful advance by Yevtushenko into universalism, a generalization of mankind which lifts his thought out of his not infrequent earlier outbursts of nationalism. His anger against injustice is unrestrained, whether it occurs in Cape Town, New York, or Moscow. The idiom of God and religion rolls naturally from his lips. He is a believer but in a universal God and a universal Man.

It is clear that the roots of *Almost at the End* and Yevtushenko's experimental film *The Kindergarten* are closely intertwined. The childhood autobiographical elements are identical with many of those which become vignettes in the prose poem and serve to unify its structure.

In many respects *Almost at the End* serves as an exemplary pilot model of the kind of literary and philosophical experimentalism that the heroes of the poetic explosion of the Khrushchev days would like to develop in the contemporary times of Gorbachev.

This book is, in its way, an act of courage akin to that which Zhenya displayed when he was shoved and kicked from a public platform by young thugs in my native Minnesota in 1972, or when he calmly waited out a bomb threat at the Cathedral of St. John the Divine which interrupted a reading by him in the winter of 1986.

Whether the risks are physical or literary, Yevtushenko confronts them and all life's challenges directly. And he's a man of passion, as this daring work reveals.

ALMOST AT THE END

I WOULD LIKE

I would like
              to be born
                            in every country,
have a passport
                for them all,
to throw
        all foreign offices
                            into panic,
be every fish
              in every ocean
and every dog
              along the path.
I don't want to bow down
                        before any idols
or play at being
                an Orthodox church hippy,
but I would like to plunge
                          deep into Lake Baikal
and surface snorting
                    somewhere,
                                why not in the Mississippi?
In my beloved universe
                        I would like
to be a lonely weed,
                    but not a delicate Narcissus
kissing his own mug
                    in the mirror.
I would like to be
                  any of God's creatures
right down to the last mangy hyena—
but never a tyrant
                  or even the cat of a tyrant.
I would like to be
                  reincarnated as a man
                                        in any circumstance:
a victim of Paraguayan prison tortures,
a homeless child in the slums of Hong Kong,

1

a living skeleton in Bangladesh,
a holy beggar in Tibet,
a black in Cape Town,
but never
            in the image of Rambo.
The only people whom I hate
                        are the hypocrites—
pickled hyenas
            in heavy syrup.
I would like to lie
                under the knives of all the surgeons in the world,
be hunchbacked, blind,
                    suffer all kinds of diseases,
                                    wounds and scars,
be a victim of war,
                or a sweeper of cigarette butts,
just so a filthy microbe of superiority
                            doesn't creep inside.
I would not like to be in the elite,
nor of course,
            in the cowardly herd,
nor be a guard-dog of that herd,
nor a shepherd,
                sheltered by that herd.
And I would like happiness,
                    but not at the expense of the unhappy,
and I would like freedom,
                    but not at the expense of the unfree.
I would like to love
                all the women in the world,
and I would like to be a woman, too—
                            just once. . . .
Men have been diminished
                by Mother Nature.
Suppose she'd given motherhood
                        to men?
If an innocent child
                stirred
                    below his heart,

2

man would probably
                    not be so cruel.
I would like to be man's daily bread—
say,
    a cup of rice
                for a Vietnamese woman in mourning,
cheap wine
            in a Neapolitan workers' trattoria,
or a tiny tube of cheese
                    in orbit round the moon:
let them eat me,
                let them drink me,
only let my death
                be of some use.
I would like to belong to all times,
                            shock all history so much
that it would be amazed
                    what a smart aleck I was.
I would like to bring Nefertiti
                        to Pushkin in a troika.
I would like to increase
                the space of a moment
                                a hundredfold,
so that in the same moment
                    I could drink vodka with fishermen in Siberia
and sit together with Homer,
                        Dante,
                            Shakespeare,
                                    and Tolstoy,
drinking anything,
                except of course,
                            Coca-Cola,
—dance to the tom-toms in the Congo,
—strike at Renault,
—chase a ball with Brazilian boys
                        at Copacabana Beach.
I would like
            to know every language,
                        the secret waters under the earth,

3

and do all kinds of work at once.
                              I would make sure
that one Yevtushenko was merely a poet,
                              the second—an underground fighter,
                                                  somewhere,
I couldn't say where
                  for security reasons,
the third—a student at Berkeley,
                              the fourth—a jolly Georgian drinker,
and the fifth—
                  maybe a teacher of Eskimo children in Alaska,
the sixth—
            a young president,
                              somewhere, say even in Sierra Leone,
the seventh—
            would still be shaking a rattle in his stroller,
and the tenth . . .
                  the hundredth . . .
                                    the millionth . . .
For me it's not enough to be myself,
                              let me be everyone!
Every creature
            usually has a double,
but God was stingy
                  with the carbon paper,
and in his Paradise Publishing Company
                              made a unique copy of me.
But I shall muddle up
                  all God's cards—
                                    I shall confound God!
I shall be in a thousand copies
                        to the end of my days,
so that the earth buzzes with me,
                              and computers go berserk
in the world census of me.
I would like to fight on all your barricades,
                              humanity,
dying each night
                  an exhausted moon,

4

and being resurrected each morning
                              like a newborn sun,
with an immortal soft spot
                    on my skull.
And when I die,
                a smart-aleck Siberian François Villon,
do not lay me in the earth
                        of France
                              or Italy,
but in our Russian, Siberian earth,
                          on a still green hill,
where I first felt
                that I was
                        everyone.

FUKU

Knocking innocence from me,
                          a kid,
they sprinkled wisdom over my borscht
                          along with the cockroaches.
Wisdom was whispered to me,
                          in a murmur,
by the fleas
          sewn into the seams
                          of my patched shirt.
But poverty is not wisdom,
                and money is not wisdom,
yet, inch by inch,
I grew up clumsily,
                in a jerking motion,
after they punched me in my empty stomach.
I used the high-flown argot of knives.
I smoked cold saliva in somebody's dropped cigarette butts.
From my guts I learned the hunger of war.
My ribs taught me the geography of Russia.
Nobody gave me
                so-called fame,
I snatched it myself,
                by the neck, like a chicken.
My soul filled up
                like a wartime train station
with screaming,
                clambering,
                          crying people.
In my soul are more than seventy countries,
all the concentration camps,
                          all the monuments,
and the pride of our era,
                          and the shame
and the card sharps
                          and the presidents.
Swallowing the epoch and choking on it,
but never puking out of squeamish disdain,

I know no less than dust or dirt,
and more than all the ravens with their doubtful wisdom.
But I grew too proud,
                        too cocky for my own good.
I became so impossibly vain
you'd think I wore a special stamp
                        across my forehead
with the confidential phrase:
                        Top Secret.
In vain I turned my nose up to the ceiling,
taking pleasure in the childish thought
that they'd bump me off soon—
                        because
I knew too much.
In Hong Kong I tried to land on a knife,
in Vietnam I flirted with bullets.
I'd been impatient to be killed,
                        to be a hero,
but they punished me skillfully,
                        by postponing my death.
And I remained alive—
                        humiliatingly—
externally unwounded,
                        hurt only inside.
They hassled and harassed me,
                        they ate me alive,
cunningly torturing me to death
                        with nondeath.
Shamefully whole,
                        I'm not decorated
with pleasant battle scars
                        or other gifts.
There may be a reason why they haven't killed me:
what if my knowledge doesn't scare them at all?
That bitter thought took away my swagger
and the remnants of my former conceit:
my deeds lag behind my inner needs;
my words lag behind my inner worlds.
If you grab life's mystery by the tail
it slips through your hands so smoothly.

The more mysteries we understand,
the more the main mystery becomes bottomless.
We ourselves have buried so much on the bottom,
and the accursed abyss of knowledge
has swallowed up such famous ships,
gobbled up such mighty states.
And I have lost myself on this earth,
from a torturing lack of talent,
feeling like a gnome crushed by the burden
of a weary and crippled Atlas.
Probably in the same way Christopher Columbus
lost himself with his desperate drunken crew,
setting sail over blood into the depths of the mystery,
the taunting mystery melting in fog. . . .

But I had no crew.

I was the only Russian in Santo Domingo, when I stood at the baggage claim and waited for my luggage. Finally it arrived. It looked like an Indian who had been tortured by the conquistadors. Its sides were in shreds, its innards spilling out.

"Damaged in transit . . ." muttered the Dominicana Airlines representative, grimly, avoiding my eyes. After that, my long-suffering leather comrade fell into the hands of the customs agent. Then whose hands were the first? Behind the backs of the customs men rummaging in my shirts and socks, the airport police chief's belly, which began practically at his chin, swayed majestically as he observed this literally touching experience. The police chief would have been a real find for the gold-loving Columbus: a gold Rolex was worn on his left hand, a gold ID bracelet on his right, gold rings with various precious and semiprecious stones on almost every finger, a gold medallion of the Madonna on his shaggy chest, a gold charm on his key ring in the form of a miniature Statue of Liberty. The police chief's face glistened as if he had smeared brilliantine on it as well as on his thick black hair. The police chief did not stoop to an interest in clothing, but he picked up a volume of my poetry in Spanish and flipped through it selectively and tensely.

"The book was published in Madrid under Generalissimo Franco," I said to calm him down. "Look at the date."

8

He was startled by the fact that I spoke Spanish, and a kind of connecting thread was established between us. He thought carefully about what to say and at last chose the simplest and most accessible:

"A job's a job. . . ."

I recalled a refrain from Okudjava's song and smiled. It was a restrained smile, but the police chief must not have expected me to smile at all. Another connecting thread.

Then his fat but agile fingers came upon a video cassette.

"That's my own film," I explained.

"Your own in what sense?" He demanded a clarification.

"I directed it," I replied, having no pretensions to the holy rights of Sovexportfilm.

"Title?" wheezed the chief, pondering the situation.

"Kindergarten."

"You have kindergartens, too?" he asked suspiciously.

"Not enough, but we have them," I replied, trying to be objective.

"What system is it?" he asked in a businesslike way.

"VHS," I replied. Another thread.

"I have only Betamax," said the police chief, almost complaining. "They keep complicating life, complicating it." And with a sigh he added, as if apologizing, "I'll have to turn the cassette over for viewing. We'll return it to you the day after tomorrow, if . . ." he fumbled. "If there's nothing in it that . . ."

"This is the sole director's copy. It's worth a million dollars." I decided to fight gold with gold. "I have no doubts about your personal honesty, but the cassette could be copied by your deputy or your deputy's deputy, and the film will start making the rounds. You know better than I about the problem of video piracy. This could end up in international court." The "million" and the "international court" made an impression on the police chief, and he hacked and puffed, bouncing the cassette in his sinewy peasant hand with its aristocratic pinky nail.

Had I ever thought that my hungry childhood of 1941 would be hefted in the scales of a policeman's palm? Along that hand I wandered, eight years old, having lost my train; on that hand the iron-tipped boots of black-market speculators trampled my violin only because I had taken—not stolen—a steaming boiled potato wrapped in cabbage leaves; on that hand a line of newly married grooms embracing their white-veiled brides came upon Siberian widows in black, holding quivering death notices in their hands. . . .

But for the police chief the film in his hand was not my life, a thing unknown to him, but merely a personal danger, well known to him, because the chair on which he sat could be pulled out from under him for lack of vigilance. That is the fate of art in the hands of the police.

"Is there anything in here against the government of the Dominican Republic?" the police chief muttered uncomfortably.

"Word of honor—nothing," I said sincerely. "I can sign something, if you want."

"No, that's not necessary," the police chief said hurriedly and returned my childhood to me.

And I went onto the streets of Santo Domingo
clutching the year '41 to my breast,
and some sweet childish fear resurrected inside me
was expecting somebody's switchblade knife.

And again I was that kid who got away from pursuers,
who didn't scare easily, who still doesn't,
jumping down from the policeman's palm, so sticky,
before his palm would become a fist.

And I went onto the streets of Santo Domingo,
clutching the year '41 to my breast,
while a Siberian ground-wind blizzard
like witch's breath followed and ran ahead.

I was followed by a crowd of sorrows,
as if a Transsiberian track ran past these Dominican palms,
and women rubbed one felt boot against the other,
lined up for bread under Columbus's bronze stare.

And behind me, through magnolia *avenidas*,
like ambassadors of old but endless war,
stood widows, orphans, wounded invalids,
carrying on their faces the unmelting Russian snow.

10

Lobsters moved their claws in stalls so easily,
pineapples lay dreaming, heaped in the shade,
and I couldn't believe that there was no line,
that people weren't writing numbers on their hands.

But through everything that seemed exotic and luxurious
and begging for color film or an easel,
came, like ghosts, unshaven faces
with a sadness of blurred, half-Indian features.

Pus oozed from eyes under straw sombreros.
Pleading, begging for at least a penny,
crooked fingers with broken nails,
flocked around me like Hitchcock's birds.

I was like a white crow. I was a stranger,
and they were tearing me apart.
The kids all tried to shine my *zapatos*,
and the whores all dragged me into the bushes.

And like a clot of universal blackouts,
near the entrance to the glittering hotel,
a Haitian boy who had fled here
tried to sell me one of his naïve paintings.

How lonely he must have been,
self-taught and not quite fifteen,
if he had escaped from Baby Doc's paradise
to this land where all artists were hungry.

Who invented this global barter market?—
"Abyss for abyss, madhouse for madhouse."
What a choice—to flee from one hell with hope
and to land in a different hopeless hell.

Here the aggression of begging poverty
clobbered me in street after street.

My sleeve was plucked, pulled, and grabbed,
and finally the pursuit wore me down.

And to the sobs of distant Siberian accordions,
and the song "Glorious Sea, Holy Baikal,"
I ran from the vile word *"Money!"*
I ran from my brothers in hunger.

For so many years the line fed me nothing
but wartime black bread eked out with wormwood—
and now at my heels, all the hungry, all the starving,
stood in line for me, as for bread.

These panting people did not know
that I myself was once a hungry kid,
that the war hit me hard,
making two childhoods and two of me.

I went into the slums. Two Creole nymphs
were my bodyguards, risking their bodies.
Their wigs from Taiwan, their shapes under tight dresses
aroused the drinkers in the sleazy bars.

Here the aggression of poverty vanished:
only the kids fought, brown skins naked,
and a cripple in rags offered me *cerveza*,
straight from the bottle, unafraid of my plague.

And they posed for my Nikon, without hiding;
they didn't reach for my pockets or threaten with knives.
I was a guest, and with me were *dos buenas muchachas*,
and no one asked me for anything.

The mothers were strict, though it was Saturday,
picking up the children playing in the dust,
and sighing, instructed, "Time to go to work. . . ."
And the children went off to beg again.

And on a fence, grinning triumphantly
like an ad for a tailor who makes tuxedos,

fluttered a torn poster: "Everything for the poor!"
and under that, a fat-faced, pre-election jester.

I asked one of the nymphs, "Who's that guy?"
and she laughed like I was crazy.
She covered her lips with a finger, which stuck to the lipstick,
and whispered a strange word: "Fuku!"

I asked carefully, "Fuku is a name?"
and she, now convinced I was stupid,
laughed harder, swayed her tight hips,
and slyly replied, "Just the opposite."

And all the poor folk, with teeth of steel
and with toothless mouths teasing the stranger,
turned to the poster and laughed,
repeating, as if blowing out a candle, "Fuku!"

The jester on the poster squirmed, one of the gang
of other thugs who promised miracles,
thugs, who with the knives of false beggars
extract votes from the hoodwinked poor.

Those guys, multiplied on every fence,
mint medals out of the people's hunger,
make bombs out of the people's hunger,
make tuxedos out of the people's hunger.

I cannot contemplate poverty calmly.
What can I do to turn my body or spirit
into the bread of salvation, into millions of crumbs,
chunks, pieces, and loaves?

In the Gothic cathedral of Santo Domingo
two sisters, two creatures of Creole nights,
unexpectedly shy, with a quiet hesitation,
lit ten candles before the Madonna.

One of the sorrowful pair explained,
as a wax drop hardened on her sleeve,

"For our dead sisters and brothers.
Ten died. We two survived."

And the expected voice from heaven did not thunder,
only a tear glistened on the Creole cheek,
and my childhood Siberian hunger
drew close to the hunger of the world. . . .

"You're the only one who can help us out, no one else can," repeated
the man with the honest blue eyes, wearing a checked shirt with a
frayed collar, and on his back a faded canvas backpack, not too full.

The man was holding a boy by the hand—a thin, sniffling boy
in shorts and white socks, with a single burr sticking to one sock.
The boy had the same blue eyes, but even brighter, shining under
his flaxen bangs.

This man, whom I did not know, had come to my Moscow
apartment early one morning. This was his story: He had been a
ship repair engineer working in Kamchatka. With his son he had
come to Moscow on vacation. They had been robbed. They lost
everything—money, papers. He had no friends in Moscow, but I
was his favorite poet and therefore his nearest and dearest in Moscow.
And so he thought that I would not refuse him if he asked for the
price of two air tickets back to Petropavlovsk-on-Kamchatka. Once
there, naturally, he would wire the money to me.

"Sonny, read Uncle Zhenya his poetry," the man said gently. "Let
him see how much our family loves him."

The boy smoothed his bangs, straightened his back, and read in
a ringing voice, "Oh, those wartime weddings!"

I gave him the money. Since then almost fifteen years have passed
and that boy probably has children of his own, yet I still haven't
received a telegram from Kamchatka. Apparently the touching little
performance had been carefully rehearsed. The whole incident with
its blackmail by sentimentality really bothered me.

My entire childhood during the war was borrowed. I was lent
bread, shelter, money, kindness, good advice, and even ration cards.
No one expected me to pay them back, nor did I promise nor could
I have promised to do so. But I am paying back, I still am.

That's why I try to lend money, even though I get burned. I've

14

begun to notice that sometimes, when people borrow from you,
they begin secretly to hate you because you are a living reminder
of their debt. Anyway, you still must give money. But where do you
get enough for everyone?

Slum children are born with this bit of wisdom:
you have to be flexible,
                              like a liana.
The children of Santo Domingo
divided up their city
                              into spheres of influence:
this one has the Carlton,
                              that one the Hilton.
What can you do?
                    You have to be clever.
The children
          who controlled my *albergo*
did not permit foreign clients a gratis exit
                                        to the street, but shook each one
gently
        as though he were a pear tree.
The children stood awaiting,
                              still as monuments,
for their clients' return
                    from brothels and taverns
with measured pleading
but perfectly transparent intent.
The children,
            working the lobby
knew by name every Bobby,
every John,
          every Frank,
independent of their rank.
A boy called Primitivo
got my name
            diminutivo
                    and immediately put it to work,
as if I were some Eugene from New York.

I remember,
        one morning
            somewhat hungover,
I came out unshaven,
          hair mussed,
and Primitivo piped up in Spanish:
"Zhenya, give money!
            Zhenya, give money!"
I did.
     He smiled a gap-toothed *gracias*.
And beneath his arm
          his bare-bellied brothers
in two voices squeaked:
           "Buenos días,"
And that day—
       I remember—
            really was good.
So we lived
       and were happy, as if in a poster,
until once,
      as a playboy imposter,
I came back in a limo sleek as a rocket
but without a *centavo* in my pocket.
And Primitivo,
        mistakenly wiser,
decided that I had become a miser,
and his two brothers
         in a sudden change,
started their little
        but painful revenge.
The moment I lay down beneath the turning fan,
under my balcony,
         like a riot
all three children sang in chorus,
"Zhenya, give money!
           Zhenya, give money!"
I smiled at first
       but later
the singing darkness scared me, like my past,

for I heard so many in that plea:
"Zhenya, give money!
                    Zhenya, give money!"
In the years of wandering and humiliations
I was Zhenka—
                    not only Zhenya.
And Siberian hoboes told me:
                    "Zhenka, listen,
you have to bear it
                    just a little longer.
Carry your cross,
                    even if you don't pray.
Hunger won't betray you,
                    and tears won't stand in the way."
The cross I bore under my skin—
                    not on my body.
Hunger didn't betray me,
                    and tears didn't stop me.
For some I am probably too rich and too famous,
but my inner self will stay hungry forever.
In the face of that worldwide hunger,
as before the horrifying abyss,
you,
    who think me a rich man,
if you only knew
                    how poor I am.
If it would save the world
                    from sorrow,
the world with so many hungry Zhenkas,
I would stop printing my poems,
I would print only money.
I would take up counterfeiting
if it could feed us one and all!
But avoid
          saccharine philanthropy.
Your cheap easy charity
                    is debauchery.
Isn't Columbus's "philanthropy"
                    more than enough

17

for poor history,
              raped and cheated?
This is how his landing ended,
with children crying,
              heartrending:
"Zhenya, give money!
              Zhenya, give money!"

"Columbus has dirty fingernails again! What am I supposed to do with that Irishman! We're going to be doing a close-up of his hands! Where's makeup!?" came the Italian screams of a cactus-legged man stripped to the waist, wearing raggedy shorts and a thick layer of sunblock on his nose.

"Maybe dirty fingernails are more macho?" the director thought out loud. His red face like burnt clay and his nose white with sunblock made him look like a cokehead.

But the camera was rolling, despite creative differences.

Banana fronds swayed lazily. They were real, but they seemed fake on the set with scenery flats of Indian hovels.

On a mat sat Christopher Columbus—an Irish actor suffering in unbearably tight boots, because he had left his own behind in Spain when they were shooting the *Santa Maria* setting sail. Next to Columbus was the Indian chief Kaonabo, a Japanese actor who bore with true samurai courage a necklace of shark teeth on his chocolate-painted neck. Columbus majestically handed the chief a string of glass beads and winked merrily at his men—American actors cheaply hired in Rome, where they did spaghetti Westerns. The chief reverently clutched the beads to his karate-honed muscular chest and with dignity handed Columbus a gift in return—a gold mask made of brass. The extras, selected on Santo Domingo's wharves from the ten-dollar whores, who were supposed to be virginal native maidens, and the pimps and lumpens, wildly painted to resemble bloodthirsty warriors, waved their straw skirts, spears, and colorful plywood shields. Hands banged on war drums to prerecorded music that came out of Gründig amplifiers.

"Open on . . . the fruit!" the cameraman roared. The cactus-legged man shoved one of the native girls in the back, and she floated toward Columbus, swinging her ass professionally and bearing on her head a platter of papier-mâché tropical fruit, even though

18

there were tons of natural fruit all around.

"Cut!" said the director funereally. "Where did the old woman come from?" And everyone suddenly saw a tiny stooped Indian woman in rags who had somehow made her way among the extras. The old woman was blissfully swaying to the music's rhythm, gulping rum from a half-empty bottle that she held in her wrinkled, desiccated hands, so like those of a child aged by someone's evil magic.

And I suddenly remembered . . . once, in a Russian movie, I had played Konstantin Tsiolkovsky, a provincial eccentric who was widely recognized after his death as a space pioneer. While filming a prerevolutionary marketplace in a little Russian town, I stood wearing Tsiolkovsky's black cloak, next to a steam engine covered with pelts of silver foxes and sables. The merchants' tables groaned with sturgeon, roast suckling pigs, jellied meats, and champagne bottles. (One of the sturgeons vanished permanently on the second day of shooting. "It fell and broke. We wrote it off," was the director's curt explanation, while local workers feasted for three days on prerevolutionary sturgeon in their Soviet canteen.) And unexpectedly a frail gray-haired old woman, carrying a net bag with two cheeses and a bottle of yogurt, entered the frame. The old woman quietly sidled between the laughing merchants in top hats and fitch-trimmed coats, between constables with gallantly curled handlebar moustaches, until she was grabbed by the ubiquitous hand of the production assistant. . . .

The cactus-legged man rushed over to the old Indian woman and led her out of camera range with a policeman's authority. The woman could not understand why those people wouldn't let her dance with them. But the false past does not like the real present to intrude.

"Not another take!" groaned the director.

"When will this all end?!" grumbled Columbus, feeling his face to see if his gray beard had come unglued. "Somebody, bring me a gin and tonic. . . ."

So this is how you've turned,
                    history!
A shoot.
          Santo Domingo.
                    The yacht club.

19

And sipping
            a gin and tonic,
Christopher Columbus de Cinema.
Between the boring takes
he sits and thinks
                about flying back to Dublin.
He says to Alonso Ojeda,
"Charles,
        we won't get too soused?"
The Indian chief from Tokyo is playing cards—
stealing just five minutes,
and false history
                in movie makeup
                            wiggles its ass
                                    to the drums.

Cowardly profit,
            how you want
to cover
        your filthy tracks.
How you want
            to make history glossy,
ideal,
    unblemished by blood.
And nonideal history, drunken,
like the old Indian woman,
is tossed away by someone's hand,
so as not to spoil the picture.
The real Columbus,
                as he burned
the cabins to the ground,
looked at them with a business eye,
as if the cinders groaned with gold.
Maybe the idea for napalm
was cleverly stolen from Columbus?
Was it nuclear war he was calling down
when he pushed a cannonball into the mortar?
He carried hunting dogs in his holds
for catching Indians
                not animals.
Boots sinking into corpses,

20

he ordered rings pulled from their nostrils.
And the greasy soot of gunpowder
settling on white plumes
turned the name Colombo black,
as if he were a cruel wizard.
And Columbus
          lay dying,
                   writhing from gout,
the former hero
          unneeded by the state,
as if the bones of all he killed
were taking revenge on his bones . . .

It was so unbearably hot in Santo Domingo that it looked as if
Columbus's statue, unable to stand it any longer, would tear off its
bronze doublet, but the grave marker in the cathedral, where, if the
sign was to be believed, the admiral's bones reposed, gave off a damp
cemetery chill. That marker was like a fingerprint file for the world,
for every tourist felt duty bound to touch it. Local black marketeers,
appearing like ghosts from behind the peeling columns, offered tour-
ists a more hospitable rate of exchange in tactful whispers. Columbus
lived in that cathedral as if in four dimensions, because in the four
corners of the cathedral several guides simultaneously told various
stories about his life to the rustling accompaniment of dollars, francs,
and West German marks. In one corner Columbus had just explained
his idea to Queen Isabella's confessor, who was pretending to be
deaf; in another he was already sending the queen gold and slaves
from the New Indies with this humane note: "And even if slaves die
in transit—not all of them face that fate"; in a third he was being
sent back, put in irons by his own cook, the shackles still bearing
the caked blood of Indians; and in the fourth, already mad, with a
pen skipping on parchment, he wrote a hymn to the metal that
destroyed him: "Gold creates a treasure, and he who has it can do
anything he wants and can even lead human souls into heaven." But
whose souls did he lead into heaven when he couldn't transport his
own there?
    Here's what amazed me: not one of the guides called the admiral
by name—only *almirante*.
    "Why?" I asked my Dominican friend.

"Fuku!" he replied with a shrug.

And suddenly a gust of wind from the sea, stale and hot, rushed into the cathedral, and whirled banknotes that it had torn from someone's hands over Columbus's vault, repeating in a multilingual rustle:

"Fuku! Fuku! Fuku!"

We are those islanders
who came in canoes
bearing branches to the sails
and watched from the boats
as mango juice streamed down the moustaches
of the hungry gods.
The white gods gave us
the pigskin of the Bible,
but that skin does not save from hunger,
and horrible is the god who
can with a sharp spur
rip open a pregnant belly.
They nailed hooks into our backs
and used hot irons on our feet,
threw us into snake pits,
strung us up,
and gave gonorrhea
to our wretched wives and sons.
We are those islanders
to whom Columbus
brought the wheel and then broke us on the wheel.
We were stupefied by rum,
killed by thunder,
thrown face down on anthills.
We were conquered by the cross
and called savages,
and promised the freedom to get drunk.
Who was more treacherous?
The most savage savagery
is civilization.
Columbus, is that why

you came to our lands,
where you dug your own grave too?
By what right
did you eat our guava
and by what right did you discover us?
Europe wasn't sleeping,
it was busy capturing slaves,
and Africa wept like a widow
when, lashed by whips,
black flesh filled
our cursed isles.
The slaves broke their shackles
and ran for boats,
but a noose on a branch awaited them.
It was during the capture of people
that the word was born,
that African word *fuku*.
Fuku is not naïve.
Fuku is a taboo
on a name that has brought misfortune.
You use the name
and trouble will follow—
that's the work of the name.
Like the rust of retribution,
fuku eats through shackles,
and the first "Fuku!"
invoked here
was on the bones of the Genoan
who rotted with his sword at his side.
No Dominican—
priest, tramp,
shoemaker with nails in his mouth,
drunkard from the tavern—
would ever say out of superstition:
"Cristóbal Colón" or "Columbus."
A Creole mother can't frighten
her kids with threats of a wolf,
so she whispers, in fear of body's wrath:
"If you don't stop crying

el almirante will come!"
In museums even sweating guides
with oily smiles
won't say "Columbus,"
but only "Come closer.
Here are the bones of *el almirante.*"
No one will utter the name.
Killers and crooks erect monuments
to other killers,
and that's clear to any fool.
But the point of folk wisdom
is to shake them out of memory
and put on all killers a fuku.
You, celebrated bones,
stop knocking at the door
of the poor man who fell asleep with a sigh,
if, vainglorious,
you creak out whose bones you are,
the poor man's answer will be: "Fuku!"
We are those islanders
who are more Christian
than all the killers in the name of Christ.
You can't scrape the injury from our genes.
Fuku on the bones of that antichrist
who came with a fake cross!

Above Seville Cathedral, where—according to the Spanish ver-
sion—the admiral's bones reposed, an enormous balloon soared from
the spire bearing the words "Viva Generalissimo Franco—the Co-
lumbus of Democracy!"

Above the heads of thousands who greeted the generalissimo, in
Seville for the opening of the 1966 fiesta, floated slogans I found
discouraging: LONG LIVE MAY 1—WORKERS' SOLIDARITY DAY, BRITISH
IMPERIALIST HANDS OFF SPANISH TERRITORY—GIBRALTAR! and there wasn't
even a hint of the antigovernment demonstration I had expected.

The generalissimo was a clever populist, master of the special art
of covering up his regime's antipeople essence with propeople slo-
gans. In this respect, he wasn't alone in the world. The generalissimo
was hailed by a crowd made up not of the people, but of the pseu-

24

dopeople: government workers grown bald from being patted on the head by the state for their loyalty; storekeepers and businessmen subsidized by national banks after a loyalty check; so-called simple people, more accurately called dupes, assured for so many years by propaganda that the generalissimo was their common father; and finally, agents in civilian clothing, their hoarse throats covered with professional laryngeal calluses from their cries of welcome.

The horses' hooves beat a melodic tattoo on the ancient cobblestones as a cavalcade of riders moved down the street: members of the royal family in national costume, aristocratic amazons in black hats with white fluttering plumes, famous toreros with glittering suits. Behind them at a speed of five miles an hour crawled a Mercedes—not with bulletproof shields, but a totally open convertible. From all sides came a shower not of bullets or Molotov cocktails, but of lilacs, orchids, carnations, and roses. In the Mercedes, head no higher than the windshield, stood a thick-set man with the smug face of a successful provincial grocer, his uniform sprinkled with petals, waving paternally with his short arms and fat, heavy fingers. When his right hand got tired, he waved with his left—and vice versa. His facial muscles did not strain themselves with a smile to woo the masses, but settled for an expression of benign governmental concern. Parents held up their children so that they could get a glimpse of the "nation's father." Many people shed unfeigned tears of civic delight. A *señora* of uncertain age burst through the police cordon to kiss the tire's greasy track.

"Viva Generalissimo! Viva Generalissimo!" the crowd roared, choking on the joy of seeing Generalissimo Franco—who in the opinion of all left-thinking Spaniards (their mouths were gagged by prison or censorship), was the murderer of Lorca, the executioner of the young Spanish republic, a spider who had enveloped the country in a web of censorship, a clever dealer in beaches, museums, corridas, castanets, and souvenir Don Quixotes. But, in the opinion of this welcoming crowd, he had stopped the fratricidal slaughter of the civil war and had even raised a placating monument to its victims on both sides. In the opinion of this same crowd, he had saved Spain from participation in World War II, making do with sending the Blue Division to Russia. They say that he told Admiral Canaris, "The Pyrenees don't like to be crossed by armies—even from the Spanish side."

In the opinion of this crowd, he was an order-loving master who did not allow striptease joints or miniskirts or erotic films or subversive compositions—in summation, he combated corrupt Western influences and extended credit to private initiative. On the request form presented to him by Spain's minister of information and tourism for permission for me to read my poetry in Madrid, Franco wrote cautiously in his round, schoolboy hand: "It needs thought." Above that stood the resolution of the minister of the interior: "Over my dead body." The readings never took place, but there was really nothing for which to blame the generalissimo.

"Viva Generalissimo! Viva Generalissimo!" chanted the crowd, and its shouts must have made Columbus's bones shudder in Seville Cathedral, if, of course, they were actually there.

The sea took its revenge:
                              it scattered
the admiral's bones
                    after his death.
Gray tangles of hair crept from the skull
and the bones began wandering the seas.
Secretly
        on the queen's orders
they were transported by caravels.
Keeping his eye out,
                     an empty eye,
at night the skeleton climbed from his coffin
and raised a periscope over the world,
pressing it to gaping sockets,
and from his decayed boots,
                           without support,
with a clatter,
               the spurs fell.
His fingers,
            fleshless,
                       did not tire:
they grabbed
            the stars
                      as if they were gold.
But they,
         grasped by bones,
turned spitefully to glass beads.

Without its plumage,
                    battered and alone,
the skull attempted to shout, "I am Columbus!"
but the wind moaned,
                    "Fuku!
                         Fuku!"
and back to the lousy hold would go
the discoverer of the false India.
From island to island the bones sailed
like uninvited guests.
It's said they are in Santo Domingo.
Of course, that is very doubtful.
Perhaps, in the vault smelling of decay,
there is just emptiness
                    and Trujillo's dust?
It's said those bones are in Seville.
Tourists poke their walking sticks at them.
And once,
          with unexpected agility,
the skeleton grabbed a stick:
apparently the tip was gold
just like the rings of the chieftains' daughters.
It's said
          those bones are in Havana,
as if alive,
          writhing in anger,
quivering and clicking, they desperately want
to discover and conquer someone else.
If the admiral has three vaults,
does it mean there were three skeletons?
Or did the thirst for fame,
                         the thirst for power
tear the bones
          into three parts?
The thirst for glory
                    is the path to ignominy,
if that glory is bloodstained
                         redder than rust.
Such is the glory that has ignominiously besmirched
                              the admiral's bones.

The Spanish conquistadors got Indians drunk on "fire water," the Indians later sharpened the pieces of broken bottles and made arrowheads out of them.

Oh, how I would like to bury forever
in the mud, beneath the remains of their statues,
the new name for killers, "occupier,"
and the old one, "conquistador."

Why did you carry chains in your holds?
Tell me, what kind of courage is it
to turn all the blank spots on the map of the world
into bloodstains?

When you were dying, Admiral,
and turning from side to side,
rasping, you tore at the blood
of Chief Kaonabo on your gouty hands.

Blood binds the world together
and the blood of the murdered chief
lay like a brand on Columbus's grandson,
who paid for the sins of his grandfather.

But my own *Santa Maria*
was an oily fish barrel on Lake Baikal.
Why am I fated to suffer this guilt?
I'm ashamed to play the good guy.

I didn't nail anyone to the cross
or put anyone behind barbed wire.
But my hands burn with the crust
of all the blood spilled by men.

The fires of the Inquisition are now legends.
Now the whole planet is an execution block,

and like typhus-bearing fleas
shivers of fear go crawling about the world.

And the Middle Ages, roaring like a bear
under somebody's tasseled banner,
reappear as a "witch-hunt" someplace
or as a *conquista* called a "peace-keeping mission."

A poet in our age is the age itself.
All the countries are like wounds on his body.
The poet is an ocean cemetery for everyone,
those in bronze and those unknown.

The poet is despised by the people
when out of pitiful conceit
he betrays the poor for his own profit
and eats at the expense of the hungry.

The poet understands in all times
that each age is ruthless,
that immortality is doomed to be part of war
as long as oppression is immortal.

The poet who has not surrendered to the Middle Ages
is the ambassador of all the oppressed.
Not eternal glory but eternal shame
to those who are glorified by bloodshed.

"Why did I become a revolutionary?" Comandante Ché repeated my
question and looked up at me as if to check whether I was asking
out of idle curiosity or whether it really was important to me. I
looked away involuntarily: I was suddenly afraid. Not for myself—
for him. He was one of those "with doomed eyes," as Blok had
written.
    The comandante turned in his heavy military shoes with metal
cleats, which, it seemed, still retained the dust of Sierra Maestra,

29

and went to the window. A large black butterfly, like a quivering piece of the humid Havana night, landed on the glimmering star of his beret, folded under the epaulet of his *verde oliva* shirt.

"I wanted to be a doctor, but then I became convinced that medicine alone could not save humanity," the comandante said slowly, without turning.

Then he turned sharply, and I could not meet his eyes, which gave off a penetrating chill—from the beyond. The dark circles from lack of sleep around his eyes looked burned into his skin.

"Do you ride a bicycle?" the comandante asked.

I looked up, expecting to see a smile, but his pale face was not smiling.

"Sometimes a bicycle can help you become a revolutionary," the comandante said, lowering himself into the chair and carefully picking up a cup of coffee with his narrow, pianist's fingers. "As a teenager I decided to go around the world on my bicycle. Once I stowed away with my bike on a huge cargo plane headed for Miami. It was carrying racehorses. I hid my bike in the hay and then hid myself. When we arrived, the horse owners flew into a rage. They were terrified that my presence would affect their horses' nerves. They locked me in the plane to teach me a lesson. The plane overheated. I was suffocating. The heat and hunger made me delirious. . . . Would you like another cup of coffee? . . . I chewed hay and I threw up. The horse owners returned twenty-four hours later, drunk, and I think they lost the race. One of them threw an empty Coca-Cola bottle at me. The bottle broke. One piece of glass still had some liquid in it. I drank it and cut my lips. On the return trip they drank whiskey and teased me with their sandwiches. Luckily, they gave their horses water, and I drank with the horses from their canvas buckets. . . ."

Our conversation took place in 1963, before the comandante's tragic, bearded face was put on T-shirts by those whose imperialist flexibility allowed them to cash in on the anti-imperialist tastes of left-wing youth. The comandante was near me, drinking coffee, talking, drumming his fingers on a book about guerrilla warfare in China, which probably was not on his desk by accident. But even before Bolivia, he was a living legend, and a living legend is always shadowed by death. He sought it himself. According to one of the legends, the comandante flew out to Vietnam with a group of comrades and offered to fight with Ho Chi Minh, but Ho Chi Minh politely declined. The comandante continued to seek death, struggling through the Bolivian jungle, enveloped in a swarm of mosquitoes, and he was betrayed by the impoverished peasants in whose name he fought, because behind him, instead of the freedom he promised, came punitive squads who killed anyone who had given him shelter. And death came into the village schoolhouse in La Higuera, where he sat at the teacher's desk, tired and sick, and his death, wild with anticipation of rewards, barked out in a military voice, "Get up!" Ché swore, with no intention of rising. They say that when they poured bullet after bullet into him, he even smiled, for this might have been what he wanted. And from his dead body they chopped off the hands with the pianist's fingers and carried them by plane to La Paz for fingerprint corroboration. Then they hacked up the body and scattered the pieces over the selva, so that there could be no grave to attract people. But perhaps, if he did die smiling, it was because he was thinking that people can achieve things in death that they cannot achieve in life. Christianity might not exist if Christ had died on a high government pension.

And now, holding the coffee cup in his unsevered hand and ruthlessly looking at me with his ungouged eyes, the comandante said:

"Hunger—that's what turns people into revolutionaries. Either your own hunger or that of others—when you feel it like your own."

Like a strange, monstrous rose growing out of stone
you blossomed out of the oil,
                    Caracas,
and beneath the hotels
                    and the brothels
sleep conquistadors in rusty cuirasses.
A girl will peel off a lacy stocking,
and some ghost on duty
curiously knocking with his nonexistent balls,
drills with obscenely trembling sword
a peephole
            in the parquet floor.
Their grandsons have erected oil rigs,

31

and race around in limousines,
                              but retribution awaits them—
that's the sword of Columbus,
                              sticking out of the asphalt,
ripping holes
              in their tires.
People dance
              on one leg,
                              not knowing where to step with the other.
Watch out:
When you burst into the bars,
don't step
on the severed hands of Ché!
In your cocktails
                  don't poke
                              your stirring sticks
into the comandante's gouged-out eyes!
In the dark night
                  in the slums of Caracas
the shade of Ché
                  clambers on the slopes.
But can the weak star of his beret
illuminate all the mists of the planet?
The ramshackle shanties, *barrios pobres*:
this isn't central, this is anal Caracas.
Down from the hills it sends shit and piss
on the conquistadors' monuments,
and down rushes
              nature's revenge
aguas negras—
              black waters—
and the smug center
                  is inundated
with black hatred,
                  black envy.
Everything that haughtily calls itself central
will be punished—
                  that is for sure!
Between the huts,

                        between the shacks—
black chomping,
                        black slurping.
That is the murmuring bacterial spawning
of the black waters,
                        aguas negras.
In that thick,
                        bubbling plasma,
we are stuck,
                        Comandante,
                                    you and I.
This is a lifetime,
                        this is forever—
mierda,
            Immoral quicksand *mierda.*
You can't get a foothold on the greedy muck
that whispers to everything living:
                                    "I hate you!"
How,
            struggling out of total shit,
can you fight
                        with severed hands?
Here even love isn't considered happiness.
Conception resembles a crime.
Something living moves in the swamps,
                                    in the darkness.
Two shadows devour
                        each other's lips.
For the hungry
                        the only food
is their kiss,
                        fierce and desperate,
and under their feet the quagmire
squeaks like a thousand rats. . . .
Oh, how terrible are the lullabies
in walls made of Pepsi crates,
where rat after rat creeps
to gnaw at a child's throat,
and their Pinochet whiskers

quiver:
      "Tasty . . .
               tasty . . ."
A horrible river,
            flooding the roofs,
rats,
    Comandante,
            rats.
And they,
          standing on their back legs,
gnaw through electric lamps
                  like someone's little hopes.
Polished rats
           to the right, to the left.
Hunger
       is always the result of theft.
Rat-rockets
          filled their bellies
with the bread of the world's hungry children.
Rat-submarines,
             teeth waiting,
are the cemetery of unbuilt schools.
Rat diplomacy
           with flicking tail,
gnaws into a mother's milky breast.
I would trade all the arms on the globe,
even your submachine gun,
                 Ché Guevara,
for a simple ratcatcher's pipe!
What pursues me around the world?
Hunger.
       Other people's and my own.
And at my heels,
          so I can't hide,
rats,
    rats from Columbus's hold.
When I see the devouring rat-ism of the world,
and all the rat-ified utopias,
I feel like someone starving to death

                         in countless Ethiopias.
With the broken lead pencil
                    of my childhood
I write a number on my grown-up hand.
I am
    number four billion and one
in the endless line for hope.
Where does this line begin?
Where it beats its frozen fists
on the door of a Zima Junction store,
and where speculators made out like rats.
The line
        has become an interminable drama,
the march of humanity
                    the slowest march.
This line stretches
            along the Amazon River
like a whispering Siberian blizzard.
This line snakes through Dallas,
                    through African deserts.
The tail of this line lies in the ruins of Lebanon.
People are desperate
for nonrat-ism
            for nonkilling!
Starving unbelievably,
                unbearably
for noncastration,
            for nonbureaucracy.
How people who are starved
                    for spirit
hate their hunger!
                This hunger is torture.
All nations get in this line together
for a loaf of freedom, even one stretched with wormwood.
And, licking the pencil and hesitating,
with a shudder
            I put a Zima Junction number
on the severed hand of the comandante
reaching out to me from Dante. . . .

35

The mighty oak door of the reception room, leading out to the corridor, was open and held in place by a precisely whittled wedge. Thanks to that clever piece of wood, the experienced secretary, as majestic as the Sphinx, in a voluptuous bright orange wig, could keep a controlling eye on the marble staircase with red velvet-up-holstered banisters, which her boss might use between her office and the side entrance.

"There's no point in waiting," the secretary said. "I've told you that she's occupied all day with a foreign delegation."

"It's all right, I'll wait," I said meekly, taking a strategic position in the reception room that gave me an excellent view of the stairs.

"It's kind of drafty," the secretary said, shivering and floating to the door, and with the toe of her elegant Italian shoe, which must have required heroic efforts to get on her huge soccer-player's foot, she lightly tapped the wedge out from beneath the door. The door, roaring with every spring, slammed shut, concealing the staircase.

"Now it's too stuffy," I said, still meekly but adamantly, and got up from my chair. I opened the door, lined up the wedge with my foot, and pushed it into its former place.

The secretary floated out of the room, bitterly rolling her eyes to the ceiling. An assistant came in, or rather, he did not come in, but purposefully placed himself in the doorway.

"Oh, don't you value your time, Yevgeny Alexandrovich? Oh, how can you . . . It's precious, your time. . . . I told you that she wouldn't be in today. You don't believe us, you take us for bureaucrats, but it's your time that I'm concerned about," he muttered gently, facing me, while all the time his left foot, slightly behind him, was clumsily trying to dig the piece of wood from under the door.

"Leave that wedge alone," I said in an icy tone.

"What wedge?" He smiled sweetly, continuing the pirouettes with his left leg.

"That one," I replied, matching his tone. "That little pine one . . . so sturdy . . . and neat. . . ." I went over to the door and pushed it in deeper.

The assistant, his whole body slackening, gasped, for at that very moment She appeared on the stairs—clearly headed for the side door. Seeing me, She took stock of the situation immediately and turned for the reception room, shaking my hand with her strong tennis hand, a lace cuff hiding the scarred wrist (scarred according to some rumors, from a suicide attempt).

"Forgive me for making you wait," She said with a hospitable, precise smile and made an inviting gesture in the direction of her office, taking off her mink coat on the way. I was fast enough to help her, and She appreciated it with a lightning flash of femininity in her preoccupied eyes. I was awed by her self-control and the athletic grace of her body. She was a very cultured minister of culture.

The secretary drifted in, still avoiding me with an injured air, and placed a tray at one end of the conference table, covered in billiard green felt.

"As usual—frankly?" She asked, pulling a Lipton tea bag (rarely seen in ordinary shops) from the steaming glass and letting it swing back and forth.

She suddenly took my hand in hers, so that the scarred wrist slipped out from beneath the lace cuff, and asked with the sincere sadness of incomprehension:

"Zhenya, just tell me, for God's sake, what's the matter with you? You're published, you're allowed abroad. You have everything— talent, fame, money, a car, a dacha. . . . I hear you're happily married. Then why do you keep writing about suffering, about shortages, about lines? What more do you need? What?"

Come with me, Comandante,
to places I used to live in,
where I did not sob "Give me!"
but I was given.

In that distant year, '41,
loud with drama,
I was a very poor boy
in a torn cap.

No matter what regal hat I wear
or shaggy fur coat,
the doorman's mafia
still takes me for a beggar with nerve.

No matter how much rustles in my pockets,
waitresses
see me as a ragged,
evil-smelling tramp.

Ironing the platform like a tablecloth
and hiding a smirk,
a porter will never in his life
drive his cart up to me.

When I sidle into a taxi,
without making a scene,
the driver, piercing me with his gaze,
mutters, "Get out!"

A dubious but charming girl once said:
"You, mister,
have something poor in your eyes. . . .
That's the reason!"

And I burst out laughing.
A fine end!
I used to be poor. I still am.
What luxury!

The only luxury of the poor
is the luxury of hell,
where there are no lying, triumphant mugs
and you don't need to lie.

The only luxury of the poor
is the luxury of juicy words
in bars, in wheelchairs,
with a whistling gob of spit.

The only luxury of the poor
is the luxury of tenderness
in pigsties and secret doorways,
in the crowd at Easter.

The only luxury of the poor
is a fight in the trolley,
but at least they don't care
if they lose their copper pennies.

If I hear a rustle in my pockets,
I send it all to hell,
and luxuriously open up my wallet,
for that luxury of spending.

I'll die the lowest of the low,
but with a feeling of paradise.
The only luxury of the poor
is the damp earth.

But faces, faces won't let me
go beneath the ground.
I so much want to share
myself—with everyone.

Everything that I have seen and will see,
everything that I know how to do,
I won't begrudge to Caracas,
to Ryazan or Paris.

They broke my bones at the marketplace,
beating the hell out of me,
but I'll give everything to Costa Rica
and to Uruguay.

Shared bread crumbs
will prolong a life.
The only luxury of the poor
is in always sharing.

The actress could not break the chunk of bread the way it had once
been broken in my childhood by a Siberian peasant woman. The
actress tried hard, but there was falseness in her fingers. And then

over my cameraman's shoulder I saw an old woman in the crowd of curiosity seekers. She had the eyes of a woman who had stood in a thousand lines. She did not need to change clothes, because in 1983 she was dressed just the way they had dressed in 1941.

"Perhaps you'd give it a try?" I asked quietly.

She took the bag with the bread and sat down on a sack leaning against the log wall of the railroad warehouse. Without paying any attention to the clicking camera, she did not simply look at the boy standing before her, but saw him and understood that he was hungry.

"Come here, son," she sighed, rather than spoke, and began untying her knotted bag. She broke the bread, feeling every bump on its surface with her fingers. Dividing it in half exactly, she offered it to the boy playing me, in a way that would not insult him with pity. And then, her left hand lightly fixing the gray strands of hair peeking out of her scarf, she held her right hand cupped under her mouth—so as not to lose a single crumb!—and licked them off, never taking her eyes from the greedily chewing boy, and finally let the pity burst out of her eyes, blazing with tormented blue. The cameraman wept, and I lost the sense of boundaries between times, between people, as if before me stood the same Siberian peasant woman of my childhood, offering me half a loaf of bread. I recognized the hand—dark wrinkles on the palm and careful, rough fingers, with a cheap aluminum ring shining thinly on one.

What could be more beautiful than the disappearance of boundaries and borders between times, between people, between nations . . . ?

In every border post
                there's something insecure.
Each one of them
                is longing for leaves and for flowers.
They say
        the greatest punishment for a tree
is to become a border post.
The birds that pause to rest
                        on border posts
can't figure out
                what kind of tree they've landed on.

40

I suppose
            that at first, it was people who invented borders,
and then borders
                started to invent people.
It was borders who invented police,
                                    armies, and border guards.
It was borders who invented
customs-men, passports, and other shit.
Thank God,
            we have invisible threads and threadlets,
born of the threads of blood
                        from the nails in the palms of Christ.
These threads struggle through,
                        tearing apart the barbed wire,
leading love to join love
                    and anguish to unite with anguish.
And a tear,
        which evaporated somewhere in Paraguay,
will fall as a snowflake
                    onto the frozen cheek of an Eskimo.
And a hulking New York skyscraper
                        with bruises of neon,
mourning the forgotten smell of plowlands,
dreams only of embracing a lonely Kremlin tower,
but sadly that is not allowed.
The Iron Curtain,
                unhappily squeaking her rusty brains,
probably thinks:
                "Oh, if I were not a border,
if jolly hands would pull me apart
and build from my bloody remains
                        carousels, kindergartens, and schools.
In my darkest dreams I see
                    my prehistoric ancestor:
he collected skulls like trophies
                        in the somber vaults of his cave,
and with the bloodied point of a stone spearhead
he marked out the first-ever border
                        on the face of the earth.

That was a hill of skulls.
                            Now it is grown into an Everest.
The earth was transformed
                            and became a giant burial place.
While borders still stand
                            we are all in prehistory.
Real history will start
                            when all borders are gone.
The earth is still scarred,
                            mutilated with the scars of wars.
Now killing has become an art,
                            when once it was merely a trade.
From all those thousands of borders
                            we have lost only the human one—
the border between good and evil.
But while we still have invisible threads
joining each self
                            with millions of selves,
there are no real superpower states.
Any fragile soul on this earth
                            is the real superpower.
My government
                            is the whole family of man, all at once.
Every beggar is my marshal,
                            giving me orders.
I am a racist,
                            I recognize only one race—
the race of all races.
How foreign is the word *foreigner!*
I have four and a half billion leaders.
And I dance my Russian,
                            my death-defying dance
on the invisible threads
                            that connect the hearts of people.

I stood at the modest Austrian cemetery in the town of Leonding
near a grave lovingly planted with pink geraniums. The headstone
with photographs would have been absolutely ordinary if not for
the inscriptions: ALOIS HITLER 1837–1903 and KLARA HITLER 1852–

42

1907. A geranium petal blown by the wind hung for an instant on the glassed-in face of the portly customs man, whose moustache seemed still to be wet from thousands of mugs of beer. A drop of the gathering rain respectfully crept along the gray hair of the virtuous, thin-cheeked frau. I did not find anything ratlike in the faces of Hitler's parents. But when I thought about what their son had done on this earth, I seemed to see a litter of rats squirming beneath the peaceful pink of the graveside geraniums.

Hitler was a field mouse that grew to the size of a rat. How did he become a world-scale rat, gnawing to death so many mothers and babies?

Against the background of the boys' choir at Lambach Monastery, young Adolf is amazing in his embryonic Führerlike pose: he stands in the back row, higher than everyone else, with a marked aloofness, arms crossed on his chest and gaze fixed on some point invisible to the others. Actually, he looks taller than the rest in other photographs, too, even though he was short. Did he stand on tiptoe? Where did that early megalomania come from?

He was one of six children. He was survived only by Paula, who died in 1960. Gustav lived only two years, Ida two years, Otto just a few months, and Edmund six years. Who knows, maybe when tiny Adolf appeared, his father worriedly said to his mother, "Judging by everything, this one won't last long either. . . ."

Maybe Adolf subconsciously remembered those conversations and came to believe in his extraordinariness because he survived?

Hitler grew up an orphan in his aunt's home. Maybe he was embittered by the coarse bread of orphanhood? Of course, there is no information that the aunt beat him or kept him locked up. . . . According to some versions, Hitler's maternal grandmother was Jewish, and they called him "Yid" at school. Is that what made him a pathological anti-Semite? But doesn't this story itself smack of anti-Semitism?

Two unhappy loves—one still in school for a girl named Stefanie, and then for his cousin Angelika Raubal, the hypocrisy of whose relatives and friends drove her to commit suicide in 1931, after which they slipped Eva Braun into Hitler's bed. But there are examples of failed love ennobling people instead of embittering them. . . . Of course, not in Hitler's case.

I think that the secret of his evil lies elsewhere.

Hitler was a frustrated artist and took his lack of recognition as a humiliation. I've seen his drawings and think that he had average professional abilities. But the combination of average abilities with an aggressive megalomania is a dangerous one. Hitler was twice rejected by the Academy of Arts in Vienna—in 1907 and 1908. There was a large Jewish community in Vienna in those days—primarily people from Galicia—and it is possible that Jewish dealers rejected Hitler's pictures or bought them cheap, not ever supposing that by doing so they were creating their future executioner.

Whatever the case may be, before Hitler became a global rat, inside him appeared a rat of frustrated vanity, eating away at his guts.

It was probably vanity that caused Hitler, who tried to dodge military service in the Austrian army, to volunteer for the Sixteenth Bavarian Regiment, because he wanted to prove with a gun what he couldn't prove with a brush—that he was worthy of glory.

In 1918 near the village of La Montagne, under attack by French mustard gas, he was blinded. When the bandages were removed from his eyes and he saw daylight again, he swore that he would become a famous artist. But on the day of Germany's capitulation, he lost his sight again, perhaps out of his tragic feelings. When he regained his vision he swore to devote his life to the struggle against the Jews and Reds who had not appreciated his art.

Actually, he lived up to his first vow, by becoming the most famous artist of death. He splashed bloody paint on the slashed canvas of the earth, erected scaffolds as sculpture, created obelisks of ruins, and was the first, even before the American sculptor Calder, to come up with sophisticated wire compositions. He forced the world to accept him as a fact, and he finally got people "talking" about him.

Hitler was a petty speculator advanced by major speculators. They used his personal morbid megalomania to unfold their speculation on a gigantic bloody scale. That's why they latched on to Hitler. Totalitarianism is the megalomania of mediocrity.

Be careful with mediocrities—especially if you see in their eyes the dangerously energetic sparks of megalomania.

And now the house where Hitler spent his childhood is occupied by gravediggers.

The stink of bordellos is a sign of collapse in any country, because in the womb of bordellos

even flabby, almost-left liberals
enjoy dreams of a strong arm.

Later, thanking them for being flabby,
this arm lifts those liberals by the scruff of the neck
like almost boneless, thinking sprats
and stuffs them into camps like packed tin cans.

Hitler knew the real price of those liberals.
Playing at socialism himself,
like a circus performer he scrambled
up along Hindenburg's drooping moustache.

Here he is, charming microphones like cobras.
Crowd pleaser. The crowd's in tears,
and fresh swastikas, like spiders,
dance on banners and on sleeves.

He shouts and stamps his foot in pique
with conquered Europe on his mind
and behind him—Röhm, like a ghost,
a butcher in creaky leggings.

Röhm is thinking: "Your role is over. . . .
We'll dump you, little Führer, very soon. . . ."
And this torchlight night plays and flickers
with reflections of fire on Röhm's scars.

And feeling Röhm's thoughts with his backbone,
merely acting berserk for the crowd,
Hitler thinks: "Don't toy with me, brother.
It is your role that's over, not mine. . . ."

Röhm pretends adoration and fealty,
not knowing that like a goose
he will be found with his throat slit
by the many-handed arm with long knives.

"Heil Hitler!" frenzied Gretchens squeal,
with curls as frothy as whipped cream,

and Hitler says with a brotherly handshake,
"What a night, Parteigenosse Röhm . . ."

Aged and heavier, the Duce, hearing the footsteps of his beloved,
takes off his glasses, and in his insomnia-sunken eyes glimmer tears
placed there for the camera by the makeup man's eyedropper. Into
the arms of this lonely, miserable man, abandoned by almost every-
one, Claretta Petacci, with the same eyedropper tears, flings herself
with a well-rehearsed movement, the mistress who did not betray
her love even when his great ideas collapsed. . . .

"What shame," cried a famous Italian director, and all the members
of the jury of the 1984 Venice Film Festival filled the small viewing
room with indignant exclamations: "Neofascist baloney . . . Manip-
ulation of history . . . Spitting in the face of the festival . . ."

Roaring fiercely and waving his pipe, which spouted ashes like a
tiny volcano, the West German writer Günter Grass lowered his
head like an ox, his eyeglasses bouncing on his nose and his mous-
tache quivering with anger.

"Resolution! Remove the film from the festival. If this were a
German profascist film about Hitler, I would do the very same thing."

Resembling a gray-haired Pyrenean eagle that has spent so many
years in exile, gripping Mexican cactuses with its claws and bitterly
gazing across the ocean at its Spanish homeland, Rafael Alberti said,
"This doesn't simply smell of fascism. It stinks of it."

"My sense of smell is in solidarity," said with soft firmness a
Swedish director who resembled a provincial teacher.

"Shocking," said Erica Jong with a shake of her curls, combining
the passion of a fighter for sexual liberation with the indignation of
a decent American housewife.

"It's not just shit . . . it's dangerous shit, because they'll eat it up
and weep," I said.

The eyes of the festival official began scurrying and quivering like
two black alarm-bell buttons. One half of his face shot off to the
right somewhere, the other half to the left. His nose traveled from
right to left and vice versa.

"*Momentito!* I share your views completely, *signori*. . . . This is a
bad film. . . . This is a very bad film. . . . This is worse than a bad
film. . . . This is shame for Italy. . . . But the administration is in

a difficult position. . . . For the first time, perhaps, we have the world's most progressive jury. But allow me this bitter joke, *signori*: progress can be attained only with the help of reaction. We will immediately be accused of leftist extremism, of being in the hands of Moscow—yes, yes, do not smile, Signore Yevtushenko! Next year our left-wing administration will be fired, and in whose hands will the festival be? In the hands of people like the ones who made *Claretta.*"

"You mean we cannot vote against fascism because by doing so we will promote fascism? It's a familiar theory," wheezed Grass with an ox's stubbornness, peering over his glasses as his face turned red.

"Unfortunately, that is precisely correct," said the official, wringing his hands. "Yes, yes, *signori*—it is shameful, but it is so." He actually turned pink with civic shame, like a boiled octopus.

The famous Italian director in an unbribable halo of gray hair turned his neck in discomfort as if suffering from an attack of osteochondrosis.

"If we ban this film, we could be accused of using the same fascist tactics," he said, looking down.

Erica Jong supported him with dignity. "Even though this does not change my opinion of the film, in general I am against any form of censorship."

"But this is not a ban against showing the film, only a proposal to remove it from the festival, for which we are responsible," Grass exploded, his glasses falling from his nose into the ashtray.

"The very word *remove* has something totalitarian about it," said one of the jury members gently, scribbling geometric figures on a piece of paper. "In Italy, we do not like such words as *ban* or *remove.*"

"The film is so mediocre that it will elicit an antifascist reaction in the audience," said another jury member.

Only the three foreigners, not including Erica Jong, voted to remove the film from the festival.

The official sighed in relief, seeing that his salary for progressive activity was safe—at least until the next festival.

But Grass was still ox-stubborn.

"Motion!" he rasped. "In that case, we must at least express our common attitude toward the film with a protest. I will write a draft."

"I will, too," I said, sensing that Grass would write something unsignable. And so it was.

"You overstress the fact that the film is 'profascist,' and that is a political accusation. Art must be above politics. ... . In Italy there is no fascism nor are there profascist feelings. Individual small groups are atypical." (Oho, it's been a long time since I had heard that word *atypical* from our severest critics!) "In Italy there never was fascism in the sense that you had it in Germany, Signore Grass—for instance, we never had anti-Semitism or gas chambers. ... . Mussolini was nothing more than a figure out of an operetta—why take him seriously?" The majority of the world's most progressive jury bombarded Grass from all sides.

They clutched at my less-harsh draft of a resolution with what seemed to be even delight. But then the collective editing began—and that was one of the worst editing ordeals I've experienced in my thirty-five years of Russian literary life.

The resolution was read from right to left and left to right, recapitulating the movements of the festival official's facial muscles, and also from top to bottom and bottom to top. Every word, every punctuation mark was weighed and mussed. First I was appalled, but then I got into the swing of it. I waited with curiosity to see how it would all end, endlessly changing, substituting, and deleting in accordance with all the criticisms, some mutually exclusive.

The final text of the resolution, which barely retained a single word of mine, was elegantly brief, like a Persian verse miniature:

We, the members of the jury of the Venice Film Festival, standing on the principles of freedom of art, which includes noncensorship, unanimously express our moral protest against the sentimental idealization of fascism in the film *Claretta*, even though we do not forbid its showing at the festival.

I read this draft, created, so to speak, by the entire creative collective, and a deadly silence reigned, except for the oxen lowing of Grass, unhappy with the resolution for being too soft.

And suddenly I realized that the resolution would not be signed even in this form.

"Do we need a collective protest at all?" The famous Italian film director broke the silence, massaging his neck with a soft groan. "Everyone can give the press his opinion separately. ... There's something herdlike about collective protests. ... I'm against lev-

48

eling individualism. . . . Besides, I'm certain that our protest will merely create publicity for the film, which otherwise might go unnoticed. . . ."

I liked that famous Italian director. I especially liked the way the girl's stormy, scornful gaze made hotels and skyscrapers explode and fly up into the air, and how colorful debris, falling from closets, soared, and how frozen, cellophane-wrapped chickens flew, escaping from refrigerators.

He himself taught me to blow things up with a look, and I blew up that room, and pieces of the table of meaningless meetings and endless pages of drafts of the unsigned resolution swirled in the air. And the tentacles of the official, flying separately from the body, admonishingly waved in the air.

"So that's what you're like—left intellectuals, defenders of freedom of speech," I said. I was upset precisely because I loved that director. "You readily sign any letters defending the right to protest in Russia, because it doesn't cost you anything, but you're afraid to sign a protest against your own mafia. . . . And I worked away, rewriting, like a fool."

The famous Italian director's face contorted and twitched, and suddenly I saw that he was aging with every word he managed to squeeze out.

"You foreigners, you'll leave tomorrow, but we have to live here," he shouted, holding his neck with both hands now. "You don't understand what that mafia is like. . . . They broke every bone in a poor *paparazzo*'s body, because he sneaked onto a set. . . . He barely survived. . . . And I still want to make a few more films before I'm found in some dark alley with my head bashed in by a black-jack. . . . Now do you understand?"

Now I understood everything.

The resolution was not signed.

When I went to a press screening of my film *The Kindergarten*, I felt a push by the little hands of those Siberian boys who during the war stood on wooden blocks to reach the machine lathes to make shells. As soon as the lights in the screening room went on I shouted out what I thought about *Claretta* and fascism. I was in a fog and couldn't hear myself speak; all I heard was the hoarse voice of the Siberian steam locomotives of 1941, blaring inside me.

And then I walked down the deserted nocturnal streets of Venice, and Claudia Cardinale's face laughed at me from the innumerable posters advertising *Claretta*, which was to be shown the next day.

A young man in a motorcycle helmet, who had parked his Harley on the sidewalk, was pressing a girl in a similar helmet against a concrete wall. The girl wasn't resisting very much, and when they kissed, the helmets clinked. When they got back on the bike, I saw a swastika on the girl's T-shirt, which had come off the wall when he'd pushed her against it. The Harley took off with a roar in the direction of the "wild" beach, taking along the swastika gripping the girl's back like a spider. I walked over to the concrete wall and touched the swastika. It was fresh.

On Hitler's birthday
          beneath the all-seeing sky of Russia
this pathetic gang of
          Moscow boys and girls
              is not merely pathetic,
an earring with a tiny swastika—the mark of a Nazi,
                a racist—
hangs from the pierced lobe
          of a wolf cub, or maybe simply a puppy.
He, a semipunk, Russian,
          with a silver-lidded overpunked girl,
whose multicolored hairdo holds a homemade swastika barrette,
stands bowlegged, in a creaking black leather jacket.
He is maintaining order.
          You won't pull the wool over his eyes.
With Nazi signs
          he stands on graves full of Nazi victims.
He hisses at a veteran:
          "Pops, bug off, give me a break. . . .
What are you griping about?—
          In India this is a fertility symbol.
We're friends with the Indians, Pops. . . .
          Friendship and peace!"
How could it happen
          that these so-called "exceptions"
could be born
          in a country of twenty million and more victims?

What allowed them,
                    or more precisely, helped them, appear,
what allowed them
                    to clutch at the swastika as at the last straw?

The same sign was over the Mathausen Camp gate
where General Karbyshev
                    on a winter day
was drenched in water
                    and was transformed
into a statue of ice and nonbetrayal.
Sidewalk pigeons
                    grumble on the square,
and in the eyes of the gray veteran—
                                    paternal anger,
and Karbyshev,
                    watching his swastika-playing descendants,
turns to ice again
                    in horror and shame. . . .

But there are names on which history itself puts a fuku after their death, so that they cease to be names.

   People tried not to say the name *Beria* even when he was alive— it instilled so much fear.

   Once, huddled like a hawk in his dark gray coat with upturned collar, he was riding in his black handmade ZIM limousine, slowly as was his habit, almost pressing against the curb. Between the muffler above his chin and hat pulled down low and through the half-shut white curtains, his gold pince-nez glittered on his hooked nose, gray hairs bristling from the nostrils.

   Merrily stepping over spring rivulets full of newspaper boats, which might have had that man's picture on them, and swinging an oilcloth schoolbag, down the sidewalk came a slender albeit too-heavy-legged, tenth-grader with a pug nose and golden braids protruding from a blue beret—to match her eyes—and a jaunty pigtail. That hawk always liked slightly heavy legs—not too much, just a little bit heavy. He signaled the chauffeur, who knew his boss's habits and pulled over to the curb. The chief of the bodyguards leaped out of the car and gallantly offered the schoolgirl a lift. She rarely got to ride in cars, and without the slightest fear, she agreed.

Later, much to his own surprise, that hawk grew accustomed to her. She became his only permanent mistress. He gave her a separate apartment, rare in those days, across from the Georgian restaurant Aragvi, and she bore him a child.

In 1952 a classmate of hers invited me to her birthday party along with two other poets, then famous only in the corridors of the Literary Institute and not yet weighed down by state decorations.

"Himself" was out of town and not expected, however two rubber-booted men with unmemorable but remembering faces stood in the courtyard, and their doubles smoked stinking cheap cigarettes on every landing.

The table was set buffet-style, unusual back then, and despite tangos and foxtrots on the Victrola, no one danced and the few guests tensely hugged the walls with their plates, heaped with almost untouched stuffed coxcombs, spiced cabbage, boneless chicken tsazivi, and other Georgian delicacies brought from the Aragvi under the personal supervision of the director—the great Longinoz Stozhadze, who resembled a retired circus strong man.

"Well, why isn't anyone dancing?" the hostess asked with forced gaiety, trying to drag people out into the middle of the room. But the space in the middle remained empty, as if "himself" had suddenly appeared there, preening like a hawk in a coat with upturned collar, and from the brim of his hat former snowflakes dropped slowly onto the parquet floor, counted out the seconds of our lives. . . .

As I was told, many years after the hawk had been executed by firing squad, she (in the almost-forgotten expression) "took up with" the black marketeer Rokotov, who was also later shot.

And so, swinging her oilcloth bookbag, a Moscow schoolgirl entered history because of her slightly heavy legs—not too much, but just a little. . . .

The Kolyma River:
                    in cold and in fever
beautiful river,
                    infamous river.
The Kolyma River
                    roars and jumps,

a liquid grave for inmates of the camps.
One night under a random roof
in Siberia I find Paris,
                    chic and aloof.
I rub my eyes,
            is this really true?
                        Oui?
It's "French Week"
                on the local TV.
Aznavour from the screen
                    sings into the room
of former camp barracks,
                    full of whispering gloom.
Could you,
        as you listen to Dalidas,
remember the watchdogs on leashes?
                            Da?
Could you,
        as you watch Gilbert Becaud,
not forget Comrade Beria & Co.?
But a nineteen-year-old driver,
                        in his truck,
hung a portrait of Stalin,
                    for good luck.
And next to this moustache,
                    a Playboy bunny attempts
to turn Siberian pants
                into tents.
"Why are you bugging me,
                    Pops,
                        with the past?
In a pair of real Levi's
            I could be
                    twice as fast."
Wake up, you silly unremembering son,
it's your grandfathers and fathers
                    you're driving on.
Barbed wire will remind you of the past,
                        as it aspires

to burst all of your stupidly speeding tires.
You won't get far
                    in any jeans
if you forget
              what history means.
If you forget the victims
                          of yesterday's sorrow
you could become
                  a victim of tomorrow.
Overcoming my sadness,
                        like an inner night,
is unending arm wrestling,
                            an unending fight.
My opponent's arms
                    are incredibly able,
pushing camp topics
                      from our table.
"Here, have a glass,
                      join our repast."
For those who don't think,
                            there is no past.
How stupid you are
                    to feel no alarm,
and to be blind followers
                            of a strong arm.
If you forget the victims
                          of yesterday's sorrow,
you could become
                  a victim of tomorrow.
In a chic dress, Mireille Mathieu
                                  is on the screen.
In Siberia such rags
                      are never seen.
If Kolyma girls could dress
                            that way,
they'd learn to sing better
                            in half a day.
The table under our elbows shakes.
My opponent fights
                    without mistakes.

54

He argues
       the camps never caused any harm,
he simply wants
          to bend down my arm.
My arm,
       why are you so weak,
like the arm of a prisoner
              who will die in a week?
But with a splintering crunch
              growing through the table top,
hundreds of dead blue arms
              come to make the wrestling stop.
And bend
       to the songs from Paris-town
that
   almost victorious arm
            down.

But all kinds of people ended up on the Kolyma, not only the innocent.

A crew was taking a break at a gold-washing dredge, and the red banner of excellence, won in socialist competition, fluttered overhead. On the grass next to the other workers sat a little old man in a patched quilted jacket. The little old man was still strong and fresh, with a merry wart on the tip of his nose. He used a hunter's knife with a fur-trimmed handle to slice neatly a lanky hothouse cucumber, not a dark one with oiled sides, but a tender green one with bumps that were patently not state farm grown. The old man took a pinch of salt from a matchbox with Gagarin's picture on the side, salted both halves of the cucumber, and without hurrying rubbed one against the other, so that the salt would not crunch on the teeth but be absorbed by the pale wet seeds. Then the little old man reached into a canvas bag emblazoned with the name of the Caucasus resort town Gagra and pulled out a bottle with a screw cap, which despite the Yugoslav vermouth label, held a clearly nonindustrial liquid with floating cloves of garlic, branches of dill, leaves of parsley, and a red cap of pepper. The little old man poured a steady stream into a white ceramic mug.

"Your cucumbers turned out real good this year, Ostapych," said one of the workers with a sigh, his eyes gazing enviously not at the cucumber but at the bottle which had dived back into the subtropics.

"Why shouldn't they?" The old man grinned, crunching and munching the cuke so that one of the seeds flew up and landed on his wart. "I have double glazing in the hothouse. . . . Steam heat—and solar . . . I don't skimp on fertilizer. . . . You know, the cucumber is like a man, it needs care. . . ."

"We know the kind of care you showed men, Ostapych—in a German mobile gas chamber in Dnepropetrovsk," a moonshine-deprived worker muttered.

"Whoever brings up the past should lose an eye!" the little old man answered gently and turned to me, as if seeking support: "I did my twenty years and you could say I've been real working class for a long time now. Why do they keep bringing up that gas van? It's not like I pushed people in—I just slammed the door shut. . . ."

"Unfortunately, he's our best foreman," the quarry director whispered grimly. "Last year his crew came in first in competition. We had to hand over the red banner. But how could we—into a Polizai's hands? We finally found a way out: we gave him a bonus, a trip to Gagra, and handed the banner to his deputy. . . . 'So it goes,' as an American said."

Betrayer of the Young Guards,
no,
    not Stakhovich
                not Stakhevich,
now lives among the Indians
and grows old unpunished.
Owner of a crummy tavern
with a sign:
        BY THE SAMOVAR,
he lives a poor and boring life
and everyone calls him
            "Don Pedro."
He wears a Catholic cross.
His family
      increases,

and his grandchildren crawl around the bar,
bare-bottomed Indian kids.
Following the local custom
                         he chews
                                  betel.
He is benefactor of the local drunks,
but when he hears his native tongue,
he shudders,
              eternally the defendant.
He dries his hands on his pants,
wipes a drop from his trembling eyes,
and shoves my record at me,
Do the Russians Want War?
"Don't put the record on! . . ."
                              "I won't! . . .
How did you find me,
                    the Judas?
What can I bring you?
                      Coming, coming . . .
Do you want the truth?
                       The whole truth?"
. . . From Krasnodon he split
to Venezuela
             via Munich,
and now
         while under the influence,
he tells me about the horrors of the Gestapo
"Now you're practically on a pedestal,
but have you ever been followed
                              even *una vez?*
Has
   a hand crank
              ever been shoved
up your *culo,*
               making your blood gush?
Has anyone splashed vitriol in your crotch?
Beaten your fingers *doloroso?*
I turned in the dead
                    at first

but they said:
               'No tricks!'
My sister,
          with me right there
                      was gang-banged.
They stuck a live wire in my ear.
I can hear only with the right.
                        The left is deaf.
Pushed against the wall, I betrayed everyone,
not all together,
                but each one singly.
What else could I do
                in that slaughterhouse?
I am *el traidor*
          of Oleg,
                of Lyubka.
Fadeyev got my name wrong. . . .
But I am not an evil spy.
I'm torn up,
          and up and down and through.
It was not I who betrayed them—
                        it was my pain."
He shows me a finger,
with a nail torn out under torture,
and asks me,
          with a toothless smile,
not to mention his name.
"What if my mother and father
                      are living?!
Let them think I'm a dead man.
Why give them this *vergüenza*?"
And the betrayer of the Young Guards
pours rum sadly
with his shaking hand. . . .

In my Pioneer period, a reader's conference was held for the school-
children of the Dzerzhinsky District (named for the founder of the
Cheka). The topic was the new version of the novel *The Young Guards,*

which Alexander Fadeyev rewrote because of Stalin's criticism.

The author was present—prematurely gray, emaciatedly handsome. Redoing the novel obviously had not been easy, and he listened to every word with visible tension, drilling the tips of his fingers into his snow-white temples, as if his sculptural former-commissar's brow was tormented by constant headaches.

The boys and girls in their red Pioneer ties, holding crib sheets, compiled with the warm participation of the teachers, gave fiery speeches about how if they were tortured by the Gestapo, they would hold out, just like the immortal heroes of the city of Krasnodon.

I raised my hand even though I wasn't scheduled to speak. There was slight consternation in the presidium, but I was given the floor.

I said, "Kids, I'm so envious, because you are so sure of yourselves. Now I have a serious defect. I can't stand physical pain. I'm afraid of shots and dentists' drills. Recently, when I had polyps removed from my nose, I screamed and bit the doctor's hand. So I don't know how I would act under Gestapo torture. I solemnly promise to the entire meeting and to you, Comrade Fadeyev, to struggle like a real Pioneer with this failing."

The majestic bosom of our principal heaved in horror. But she courageously controlled herself, at the last second replacing a cry of civic outrage, which was pushing its way through her modestly lipsticked lips, with a deep pedagogic sigh.

"That boy is the shame of Dzerzhinsky District," she said. "I hope that other pupils will give a worthy rebuttal to this hostile enemy sally."

To my surprise, Kim Karatsupa, nicknamed Tsupa, who sat at the desk behind mine and always copied my literature essays, jumped up. Tsupa was transformed. He walked to the tribune not in his slouching, swaggering street manner, but almost at a march, with military bearing. Tsupa smoothed the red whorls of his hair and spoke in a voice that was no longer a Pioneer's but a troop leader's.

"As Korolenko said, 'Man is created for happiness as a bird is created for flight.' But are cowards, who fear our Soviet dentists, capable of flying? Such cowards were ruthlessly condemned by Gorky: 'He who is born to crawl will never fly.' The cowardice of eels is unbecoming to us, the descendants of the Young Guards. We, the Pioneers of class 7B of school 254, unanimously condemn the be-

59

havior of our classmate Zhenya Yevtushenko and think that the question should be raised of his membership in the Pioneer organization."

"Why do you say unanimously? Speak for yourself." I heard the voice of my comrade-in-arms of the soccer fields, Lyokha Chinenkov, but his protest was drowned in the general applause.

"Wait, wait, children," Fadeyev said in an unexpectedly high and young voice, as he stood up. His face was suffused by an unnaturally bright, feverish blush. "You could throw out the baby with the bath water this way. . . . You know, I liked Zhenya's statement. It's very easy to beat your chest and declare that you can put up with torture. But Zhenya frankly admitted that he is afraid of shots. I, for one, am too. Come on, now, be brave, everyone who is afraid of shots raise your hand!"

They laughed and a forest of hands went up. Only Tsupa's hand did not go up, but I knew that when we were getting our smallpox vaccinations he gave another kid a ticket to a big soccer game to take his shot from the nurse.

"The coward is not the one who expresses doubts about himself, but the one who hides them.

"Bravery is frankness, when you openly speak of others' defects and your own. . . . But you should still start with yourself," Fadeyev said with a sad smile.

The audience that had just applauded Tsupa now just as noisily applauded the writer.

The majestic bosom of the principal heaved in relief.

"Our dear Alexander Alexandrovich gave us all an example of a healthy attitude toward one's defects, when he accepted comradely criticism and created a new, much better version of *The Young Guards*," she said.

Fadeyev drilled the tips of his fingers once again into his snowwhite temples. . . . But the bullet with which he ended his own life was still a long way off.

My oldest son
              digs at the carpet with his running shoe.
He is unknown
              to me, his father,
                      and to himself.

60

What will he be?
                Who?
                        At sixteen
he is
    a yet-unfound answer.
My oldest son stands at the parent-teacher conference,
my oldest son,
                my silently boldest son,
like all withdrawn children
alone.
He's slow-witted,
                even though he's fatally young.
He has this damned habit
of being silent—and that's it.
His irritated teachers
nicknamed him The Silent One.
But even in his silence he's prickly.
He went and got a semipunk haircut,
and in class,
                her metal tooth gleaming meanly,
the teacher cried:
                "Fascist!"
Who gave this teacher the right
to sound a false civil alarm
and kill a nonkiller—just a child—
with the despised name for killers?
Oh, if the fascists' victims were to rise from the grave
they, perhaps, would call her a fascist. . . .
But I must be calm here.
I am not objective.
                I'm his father.
My oldest son—
            he's far from an angel.
As I wrote about myself:
                "shy and arrogant."
They forced him to shave his head,
                and like a shaved porcupine
he looks at his teachers
with the last of the needles
                in his eyes.

The Silent One,
          one of the school's rebels,
he stands
          a mute anthology
of grammatical and moral mistakes,
but still, he's not just anybody's,
                    he's mine.
They tell me with mournful expression:
"He has a hobby—
               not answering.
Well, answer, Petya,
               get used to it!
Talk at least when your father is here!
Your son is like a deaf mute.
He has a hatred for us, his teachers.
Just yesterday we were studying the image
of Raskolnikov. . . .
                    Your son was silent again.
My question was clear.
                    Tell us, this time,
about Raskolnikov's terrible crime.
But a mangy cat must have gotten his tongue.
Noisy punks are nasty,
               but nastier still is a silent punk.
His shyness isn't innocent.
                    He is insultingly shy."
Then he dug into the carpet even deeper,
and got revenge for his shorn locks:
"Because in the question you posed
you already had given me the answer. . . ."
And that started it—
               screeches and screams:
"I asked the way we are supposed to,
following the methodology of Marx,
the clear rules of the Ministry of Education. . . .
What are you grinning about, boy? . . .
Now do you see what your son is like?"
                              "I see."
And truly,
          I suddenly saw him.

62

. . . We parted after that "useful talk."
He carried off silently through the crowd
the stinging ache of an unfound answer
and teenage acne on his exhausted face.
I'm a Silent One, like him
                                despite my skill with words,
a Silent One
                    dressing my naked silence in noisy nonsense,
repressed,
             as lonely as a teenager,
but without a father.

I have two other sons—Sasha and Tosha. I'm not called to parent-teacher conferences on them yet because Sasha is only six and Tosha five.

When I was teaching Sasha to read, things weren't going too well, but—and this was Freudian, obviously—he instantly read aloud the word "skirt." Like the majority of children on this earth, my sons are constantly around skirts, and not around my unruly trousers, which are always wandering off somewhere. Sasha began walking on time and talking on time. Sasha is a strange mix of explosive energy that scatters everything in all directions and of unexpected attacks of pensiveness. He can turn the house upside down and then grow still, forehead pressed against the rain-streaked window, and think for a long time.

Tosha suckled poorly, did not grow, lay motionless. The fontanel did not grow over.

"A bad boy. Very bad," rasped a famous neuropathologist, as she hopelessly shook her flawlessly white cap.

The vicious word *cytomegalovirus* entered our house.

But my English wife Jan refused to give up.

She did not let Tosha die, did not let him not move. She talked to him, even though perhaps he understood nothing. Though they say that children hear and understand everything, even when they are in the womb.

Early one morning Jan shook me by the shoulder, her eyes brimming with tears of joy:

"Look!"

63

And I saw above the side wall of the child's bed, raised for the first time, like a periscope, the blond curly head of our younger son, his eyes nearly reasoning now.

The cytomegalovirus had done its work: it destroyed part of the brain cells. But indomitable Jan, with her Victorian stubbornness, dug up the latest system of physical therapy, in which three people move his arms and legs, do not let the child rest, but force him to move himself. Unceasing labor. Eighty exercises from ten in the morning until six in the evening. This activates other cells to take on the functions of those that have been destroyed.

Helpers appeared. Some were capable of only splashes of help and quickly evaporated, having done a one-time good deed. I noticed that many people can be volunteers only when pressed by society and are incapable of voluntary volunteer work. But there were others, who worked like oxen.

Of course, Jan herself. Zina, the guardian angel of our family, the former nurse from Kaluga, to whom Tosha said his very first "Zee."

The Tatar geodesist Valentina Karimovna, with her stealthy nomadic walk and prune-black eyes—"Kee." The Ukrainian Vera, defending her Ph.D. on child education in Japan, even though through circumstances beyond her control she has never been in the Land of the Rising Sun—"Ve." Marian, a psychology graduate student from Siberia, descendant of exiled Poles—"Ree." A former waterpolo player, and now simply a good man—Igor. An Abkhazian student, Valera, secretly writing poetry, who will never make a poet but will make a marvelous father—"Le." Resembling both the legendary folk hero Ilya Muromets and the millionaire Savva Morozov, who supported a Bolshevik underground organization, chauffeur and billiards player Vadim, who brings presents of bronze candlesticks he has won or a jar of marinated mushrooms from his hometown of Yaroslavl (where his friends missed him)—"Dee." My oldest son, Petya—"Pe." The most disciplined helpers were the British students from the Institute for Russian for Foreigners, who sang Tosha's favorite song to him during the exercises, "Baa, Baa, Black Sheep," whose only rival in Russian is "Crocodile Gena." Tosha called them "Dzh," "E," "Roo," and "Meh." And the difficult name Djuna he magically pronounced right off the bat.

An international brigade was formed to set the boy on his feet. This international brigade warmed him up, molded him the way a sculptor molds clay. It was sculpting a person from him. And the grateful little person diligently crawled on the floor, blowing at lit matches looming before him, wheezed and clambered up and down steps, rolled from side to side, flew up to the ceiling on rope swings, huffed and puffed in a transparent oxygen mask, and his mother's violet eyes gradually began to think, and his legs, once as clumsy as a wooden bull's, grew stronger, sturdier, and steadier.

But supervisors and lecturers appeared in our house, too.

They were horrified that the child was playing with matches. Wide-open windows made them shiver: we were undermining the very foundations of child care. And one lady, a former head of the banner department at the so-called Cultural Products Store, who had come to see if we needed a "domestic engineer"—she did not want to use what she saw as the demeaning term *housekeeper*—tragically flung up her hands when she saw Tosha's gym apparatus and rings screwed into the ceiling.

"Well, excuse me, but this is just a medieval torture chamber. The child needs peace and quiet and a high-calorie diet!"

But the others went on working with Tosha, and Larisa, a speech therapist with sad, biblical eyes, extracted new sounds one by one from behind his teeth with a magical metal rod with a ball on its tip.

And the day before yesterday, when we stealthily stopped supporting him by the elbows, Tosha jumped on the old cot trampoline all by himself for the first time and said the difficult word *"Jump!"*

I want to raise Petya,
               and Sasha,
                       and Tosha,
without dumping them on their moms,
but if I abandon others,
I abandon my own.
I want to raise up the orphans of Cambodia,
                               Nairobi,
to save them from missiles.
Strange children,
               like strange peoples,
do not exist.
I want to raise kids from Addis Ababa,

give them all something to eat,
to whisper to a little Zulu:
    "Would you like
to read some Shakespeare?"
And maybe hunger in Bangladesh
will kill that very peasant child
who could have brought a common hope
to the family of man.

The project for social paradise is tempting,
but it is a great shame
to adopt all the children of the world
and neglect your own.
Avowed love of humanity sometimes masks indifference:
Am I living the right way?
Embracing humanity—
                    that's more beautiful
than just embracing your own wife.
I'm busy with the planet,
                    harassed,
                            spread around,
I'm no husband—
                I'm the family disgrace.
Your son,
        if he's neglected—
                        is abandoned.
He is
    an orphan.
Of course, we must fight for children's souls,
we must,
        we must. . . .
But what, if under our edifying shell
we have no soul?
The teacher is a doctor,
                        not a sermonizer,
and school is a maternity ward.

First you earn the right to teach
and only then you teach.
We have to fight for children's souls,

but how?
Toy guns are repulsive
                        in children's hands.
They must be unthinkable.
We must fight for children's souls
                        and for ours
with inoculations of shame,
preventing the birth
                        of a führer,
                                of a duce,
of any hawks.
But before rushing into battle
for children's souls—
                        we, grown-up children,
must clean up our own.

In 1972 in St. Paul, Minnesota, I read my poetry to an audience of
American students in an indoor stadium, standing in a boxing ring,
from which the poles and ropes had been thoughtfully removed.
Suddenly I saw young people—about ten of them—running toward
the ring. I thought that they wanted to congratulate me, shake my
hand, and I stepped over to the edge of the ring. Only at the last
moment did I notice that their faces were not at all congratulatory,
but hard, businesslike, and they weren't carrying flowers. A multi-
voiced "Ah!" ran through the audience, for they could see what I
couldn't: a few more young people had jumped up into the ring and
were running up behind my back. A sharp push in the back knocked
me down, right under the feet of the "congratulators." It was all
worked out with timing and efficiency. They began kicking me with
lightning speed and accuracy. The only thing I remember is the
cleats of a hiking boot with a strawberry chewing-gum wrapper
sticking to it, which rhythmically struck my ribs like a hammer and
which seemed gigantic to me at the time. And also: through the
flicker of feet kicking me in the gut I saw the feverish flashes of a
young female photojournalist who had fallen to one knee and was
photographing my beating as efficiently as I was being beaten. My
friend and translator Albert Todd rushed over to me and shielded
me with his body. The actor Barry Boys grabbed the microphone
stand and used it like a cudgel, accidentally knocking out the tooth

of an innocent policeman. The audience sprang into action against the attackers, and even when they were being held, they convulsively went on kicking the air, as if trying to finish me off. The attackers turned out to be USA- and Canada-born children of people who had collaborated with Hitler, as if the fascism that had not reached Zima Junction during the war was now trying to get me in America. Reeling, I got up into the ring and read for another hour or so. I did not feel any pain, strangely enough. At the reception afterward, the young photojournalist came up to me. The straps of her Nikon and Hasselblad were entwined like snakes around her whittled swan-like neck.

"Tomorrow my pictures will be seen all over America," she said consolingly and at the same time proudly.

Perhaps, as a professional she was right, but for some reason, I didn't want to talk to her. The professional instinct in her was stronger than the human instinct—to help. And suddenly I felt a terrible pain in a lower rib, so strong it racked my body.

"There's no break," the doctor said, examining an X ray made in the nearest emergency room. "There is a fracture. . . . I think that they hit an old fracture. . . . Were you ever in a car accident or some other incident?"

And it came back to me. Instead of the cleats of the hiking boot with strawberry gum wrapper I saw above me, also rising and falling on my ribs, the heel of a speculator's boot with a shiny metal half-moon lift, when I was beaten in a marketplace in 1941. I told the story to the doctor and saw something resembling a tear in his unsentimental eyes.

"Unfortunately, we don't know very much in America about what your people and your children lived through during the war," the doctor said. "But I saw what you told me as vividly as in a movie. . . . Why don't you make a film about your childhood?"

That's how the film *The Kindergarten* began in me—from a kick on an old fracture.

They're hitting an old fracture
they're hitting me—
                    a kid,
they're hitting me—

                    a young man,
they're hitting me—
                    almost gray,
declaring war on me.
Fascists, speculators
                    hit
all the living and the young,
with their giant boots,
trying to kick
                    talent
in the gut.
They're hitting an old fracture,
butchers
         and bakers.
They're hitting not only the past,
they're hitting
                    the future.
The Black Hundreds are everywhere.
They dream of an atomic pogrom,
like an anti-Semitic pogrom,
with nuclear axes.
Under their feet are the children.
In them, they instill fear
and terror on the planet
and terror in the skies.
They're hitting ideas,
                    countries,
trampling nations into dust,
hitting so many old wounds
of the tortured earth.
But in any pogrom,
free of blackjack or knife,
out of all my fractures
I'll create inviolability.
It's all right that I'm spending so much time
fighting the Black Hundreds.
I haven't broken . . .
                    I won't break
from a fractured rib!

"What fools," laughed Pablo Neruda, looking through a fresh issue of the newspaper *Mercurio*, where once again he was being dragged through stale mud. "They write that I am a two-faced Janus. They underestimate me. I have not two, but thousands of faces. But they don't like any of them, because they don't resemble their own faces. . . . Thank God."

It was an unusually snowy winter for Chile, 1972, and above Pablo Neruda's house, which looked like a ship, sea gulls wheeled and screamed, mixed with the anxious, warning snow. . . .

There is a third choice—to choose nothing,
when two lies are being slipped to you,
not to change, in someone's dirty games,
into an ass licker or a slanderer.

It is more honest to die in a ditch
than to prefer the dubious honor
of escaping from your own bastards
only to be embraced by bastards abroad.

It is shameful for a true writer
who is proud of his unrecruited soul,
to break with homemade reaction
just to be reactionary elsewhere.

When your enemy is a jackal, the shark is not a friend.
There is a third choice: amid all the biting,
to sit between two chairs, if both,
in their own way, are dirty.

I despise licking both asses.
I consider it equally foul
to fawn, bowing your back before your native country,
and to turn your back indifferently on your homeland's pain.

General Pinochet's arm did not seem strong to me when I shook his hand: it felt boneless, bloodless, and characterless. The only unpleasant memory is of a cold, damp palm. In my yellowed notebook

70

for 1968, after a reception in Santiago given by one of the officials of Lan Chile, this is one of my brief entries on the guests: "Gen. Pinochet. Provin. Hand cold, damp." I think he and I spoke about something, holding glasses filled with one of the most marvelous wines in the world—"Macul." If I could have foreseen who he would become, I would probably remember more. The second time I saw him was in 1972, on the tribune in front of La Moneda Palace, where he stood behind President Allende, who spoke too urgently of the loyalty of Chilean generals, as if trying to convince himself. Mirrored sunglasses protected Pinochet's eyes from the klieg lights that struck his face.

The third time I saw Pinochet was in the spring of 1984, when I was traveling to Buenos Aires through Santiago.

The general's self-satisfied but rather tense smile looked down at me from an enormous portrait at the airport, as if to say, "And you took me for a provincial." Under Pinochet's picture was a newspaper stand, which did not sell a single Chilean newspaper. When I asked the vendor why not, she looked around and whispered confidentially:

"They have almost no text . . . just white columns—censored . . . even in *Mercurio*. . . . That's why we don't sell them. . . ."

And next door, in a souvenir shop, I shuddered as I saw a cheap, mass-produced engraving with Pablo's profile.

The petty people who had killed the great poet were now selling him.

On El Puente de los Suspiros,
on the Bridge of Sighs,
I,
   like my own ghost,
                    loomed over the gurgle of gutters.
No one sighs here at night anymore.
The old sighs
            expire.
A knife keeps watch over every royal palm.
Being a ghost is easier—
                    they won't stab you.
In a former life
            and in a former era
with my former

71

almost-beloved,
we once eavesdropped as others sighed
over Lima.
And we sighed too
uninhibited and innocent,
and the whole universe
                    poured
light blue over our skin.
And even sleeping cars
sighed with a creak,
                    and a squeak. . . .
We understand each other's sighs,
and that means we loved.
Absolutely no Ché Guevarista
inhaling freedom and space with your sighs,
you did not fear risk in love—
and that was your revolution.
Like a sigh
          you vanished,
                    Raquel.
Your ancient name from the Bible
was sucked up by nowhere and nothing
as if by Bolivian swamps.
I lost the path myself.
                    I feel only half fulfilled.
Like Raskolnikov,
               grimly quiet,
I returned to the murder scene
of our sighs—
          yours
               and mine.
It's not you I am with.
                    I am no longer me.
That's two switches,
               two substitutions.
Mangy cats are the only ones who sigh
on the mossy railings of the bridge.
And neither sighs
          nor mews
will help.

72

Total vacuum.
I fought against walls,
                              against swampiness,
but always against something solid,
                                        no matter how liquid.
I am surrounded by quagmires
                              and quacks.
The most liquid thing
                    is a vacuum.
But as I hit my face against the vacuum walls
I see
     that the vacuum is the hardest.
It considers everything that sighs as edible,
and the vacuum swallows even screams.
The bridge is dead,
                    hanging crooked,
dressed in green unwhispering moss.
If people don't have the strength to cry out,
they can still sigh
                    at least.
Man falls apart,
                dissolves,
if he doesn't have strength for a sigh.
Has sentiment been
                      trampled to dust
and are the only sanctuaries of sighs
prisons,
          hospitals,
                    and churches?
Have people forgotten how to sigh?
Are we afraid that by freely expanding,
our chests will strike bayonets,
                                as in Chile?
Any homeland dropped into the unsighing mud
will turn
         into Pinochetland. . . .
On El Puente de los Suspiros,
next to your shadow,
                    Raquel,
I feel knives behind my back

73

and bayonets
         and rockets.
Only the sea sighs with a rumble,
and winos sigh
         with a laugh,
pretending
      that things aren't
           so bad,
which is why they don't need to sigh.

Imperialism is the manufacture of volcanoes.

I was in the bunker in which Somoza had hidden when the heated lava of revolution approached Managua.

The bunker, to my amazement, was not underground at all. The gray barrackslike building concealed several rooms—study, dining room, bedroom, bathroom, and kitchen. There was even a tiny Japanese-style garden.

All this, for some reason, was called a bunker.

"Touch it," said the captain accompanying me, and smiled. I tried one plant, then another: they were all plastic. An antipeople dictatorship is a plastic garden: no matter how much the court toadies admire the fruits of the dictatorship, they cannot be eaten or smelled.

There is a bullet hole in Somoza's leather armchair: it was put there by a Sandinista, who shot in anger at not finding the tyrant in his lair. I was told that the night the bunker was taken the soldiers slept here, without taking off their shoes—some in Somoza's alcove, some on the couch, some on the floor. A line formed to use the bath with its whirlpool. And a homeless woman with a child snoozed right in Somoza's chair, and the child diligently dug at the bullet hole, pulling out the stuffing with his small finger.

I was amazed by the total absence of books in the bunker.

"He did not even read newspapers, because he knew ahead of time what they would say."

Never
      would I have seen you,
                Nicaragua,

either awake
                or in my sleep
if I did not have a heart,
                                wounded,
                                                but intact.
Their heartfelt feeling for the people
was expressed by drunken killers
as they cut out the heart
                                of a rebel
with a dull police cutlass.
But, enveloped by breaths,
                                as by smoke,
the heart went on beating, a taut lump.
The dogs' hair bristled
when they tossed the heart to them.
In its last dying moment
beneath the blood-spattered boots
the heart beat
                with a longing for freedom—
which perhaps is the only freedom
                                        we have.
You cannot hide blood
                in a safe.
Blood—
        on mink coats,
                        uniforms,
                                tuxedos.
There is no such thing as a great dictator:
all of them are inflated nothings.
On dishonesty,
                on half-truths,
on Pompeiian banquet tables,
on police,
        on the army,
                        on cowardly voting hands
stand the thrones of all dictators.
No,
    it's not for you to speak of human rights,
excisers of human hearts on dark nights!

Is justice
        only retribution,
gagged mouths,
                zealotry,
                        fear?
Among the rights of man
                        is the right
to an unexcised heart.
Freedom has fewer faces
                        than bondage,
but people's faces plus uprising
                        equal hope.
There are no
        dictators who can't be overthrown.
There are only
        ones overthrown too late.

After the fall of the military dictatorship in Argentina, everything that had been banned surfaced at the 1984 book fair in Buenos Aires. For the first time in so many years the stands were filled with former illegal literature—Marx, Engels, Lenin, José Martí, Ché Guevara, Fidel Castro. The avalanche of freedom carried sex garbage, too. Kropotkin and Bakunin stood near an illustrated history of brothels, Mao Zedong with the Kamasutra, and Trotsky and Bukharin with the Swedish best seller *Confessions of a Lesbian*. The Argentines practically tore Italian writer Italo Calvino into pieces with delight, when, during a readers' conference, he dropped in passing the slightly masochistic and, in Europe, almost banal phrase of leftist intellectuals, "We've used up all our lies. Time to stop." Unable to understand the flowers they tossed at his feet or the bright red lipstick marks left on his cheeks by enthusiastically weeping Argentine women, Calvino merely blinked in bewilderment. He simply must have forgotten or had not known that just a year ago, whenever more than two or three people gathered in the streets of Buenos Aires, they were arrested and often would disappear without an investigation or trial, shot or suffocated in secret corridors or empty lots or drowned in the sea. In many instances their corpses were tossed into concrete mixers and immured in the concrete foundations of new hotels and

banks. This gave rise in Argentina to the horrible word *desaparecidos*—
"the disappeared."

Thousands lined up to see the first uncensored political film made
in Argentina, *Beso de fuego* (*Kiss of Fire*), based on the screenplay by
the Uruguayan émigré Mario Benedetti. When the hero—a moral
degenerate but one suffering pangs of conscience—says something
like, "All our newspapers are good for is wiping our asses," the
audiences applauded and stamped their feet.

The halls of the book fair were flooded with people who had
come with huge bags and even burlap sacks to buy once-banned
books. To get a snack, you had to stand in line for at least an hour
and a half. At this feast of the mind, I got quite hungry. When a
paper plate with a roll holding a steaming hot dog and a splash of
golden mustard was carried right under my nose, practically touching
it, I licked my lips. Unexpectedly, the hand holding the paper plate
took the hot dog and with astonishing casualness shoved it right in
my mouth, so I could take a bite.

"Only half, *campañero*," a low, almost masculine but still-female
voice said just in case.

Greedily chewing the unexpected gift, I saw before me a very tall
woman, almost my height, with streaks of gray in her black hair,
and a rucksack strapped to her powerful shoulders. The bag, stuffed
with books, showed their sharp edges. The woman had stunned me
with her almost Siberian and gruff compassion for a hungry man.

We introduced ourselves. Her name was Magdalena. She was a
rural schoolteacher who had come from a distant mountain province
to buy books for the school library.

I invited her to a literary café and on the way glanced at her
surreptitiously with the eyes of an almost-retired womanizer. Mag-
dalena was around thirty-five. She was beautiful in her own way,
even though everything about her was rectilinear, rough, and en-
larged—words, gestures, hands, and feet. Yes, about her legs. With-
out stockings, scratched apparently by mountain brambles, dressed
in dusty mountain boots, they were tanned, well proportioned, and
long, though rather too sturdy, like Doric columns. Her knees were
especially adorable, independently sticking out beneath her canvas
skirt with folk embroidery—solid, powerful, like the foreheads of
two small elephants. She caught my eyes and laughed—not angrily,
but not approvingly.

The walls of the literary café were hung, as if with legalized proclamations, with the verses of poets who had disappeared without a trace during the dictatorship. Magdalena, leaving her wine untouched, got up, put her rucksack on the floor, and slowly walked along the walls, reading, her lips moving silently. Then she sat down and drained the full glass. Nothing embarrassed her, and that was her charm.

"I knew many of these poets personally," Magdalena said.

"You went to their readings?" I asked.

"No, I arrested them," she replied.

I am telling you this,
I, Magdalena.
As you see,
       I am not up to my knees in blood,
and knees like this are appreciated
by you skirt chasers.
We were not allowed to wear
                   any "minis,"
but I did not stoop
          to official "maxis."
And my knees stuck out like two terrorist mines,
above my boots in government polish.
And when I checked in Buenos Aires,
for enemies of the state,
            enemigos subversivos,
I liked
    that the mob feared me
and at the same time
           eyed my knees.
I was tall,
      and they teased me in school,
and bitterness made me a stoolie,
and inflamed with desire to save Argentina,
in my reports I painted
          a horrible picture,
where in a school conspiracy
             even the first graders

wrote in code
            on their pink blotters.
I was noticed.
                I was given a code name.
Dealing with the police
                    became a habit.
But I found
            being an informer morally demeaning.
I wanted
        a change of status.
And I began,
            by controlling the Rio del Plata,
saving Argentina
            on a police salary.
I dreamed of being part
                of a detective novel.
I was still young,
                still pretty,
and I dried my shoulder belt
                    over the gas stove,
so that it would creak
                even more scarily.
I entered the police force
                out of conviction,
and partly
        out of hatred for institutions,
but the police
            turned out to be an institution too,
and in the police force
                it was just one ugly mug after another.
I was
    a patriot
            and a black belt in karate,
and none of the chiefs made passes at me,
though they did rape me with their eyes,
but that happens everywhere,
                    as you well know.
Our agents
        branded as agents

everyone
        they considered an intellectual.
Which thinkers didn't I arrest?
Perhaps only Aristotle.
I would break like a tank
into apartments
           earmarked earlier,
and my joy
        at the government trust and confidence
would make my holster dance on my hip
                in a tango.
But I noticed
        that during searches
my valorous colleagues
pocketed cassette players—
            and video machines—logically,
and that
     offended me
        ideologically.
And I gradually realized without effort
what not everyone is given to understand—
how disgusting
        are the servants of the state
and how *simpático*
        are the state's *enemigos*.
And once a very nice
        "subversive element"
smiled,
     pitying me with his eyes,
           as in a sad prophecy.
"Eh, *muchacha* . . .
        One day maybe your grandson
will come to meet a date
        not just at anybody's
           monument but under mine."
He said it, perhaps, not too modestly,
but when they took him not to the prison,
but to the concrete mixer,
and tossed him in,

concrete mixed with blood—
for some reason I believed him.
He was a writer.
                    I kept a slim volume
                                from the confiscation,
and when I read it—
                    I wept,
                            as if a dam had been broken,
for I understood
                in my belly, never once pregnant,
that men like him
                were the true saviors of my Argentina.
Another writer
            was struck on the back in my presence
and put up against the wall,
                        but they didn't shoot him,
                                            the bastards,
they smeared his body
                along the wall
                            with a Studebaker car
so that bloody chunks of kidney
                            spattered the radiator.
They all disappeared without a trial.
                        They all disappeared
                                    without a trace.
Damning my ignorance,
                    patriotic fool,
I left the police
            and vowed forever
                        to teach literature to children.
And now I pay for my sins
in a village school
                where mountain butterflies
                                dive into our windows,
and I read to peasant children
                        the poems
of the disappeared—
                los desaparecidos.
And at night

I writhe on husbandless sheets,
with my silly knees,
                    and meaningless legs,
and the local pharmacist
                    creeps into my bed
and hurriedly pumps,
                    without removing his tie.
Even naked
          I can't pull the police uniform from my skin.
So that my children and the pharmacist's
                              will drown in my belly,
I swallow a double dose
                    of birth control pills,
while boredom and loneliness swallow me.
Some dream
          of creating police order
at least in their sleep,
                    shouting at everyone:
                                        "Freeze!"
But every day
          I choke on hatred
for every policeman
                    on the face of the earth.
I hate
     when a child is lectured by a hypocrite father.
I hate
     when teachers
                    smack of police.
This I say to you,
               I, Magdalena,
                         former policewoman,
and, unfortunately,
               former woman, too. . . .

Exactly in the middle of the Amazon a ship was burning.

   The ship was small, scruffy, under the Ecuadorian flag. People
rushed around the blazing deck. But they were afraid to jump into
the water, because the Amazon is full of piranhas that can strip a
body down to its skeleton in a minute. The two lifeboats that were

lowered capsized because they were overloaded, and not one person swam out. The tragedy of the people left on board was that the ship was burning right in the middle.

Several Indians on the Peruvian side, where I was, hurried to their canoes, but the police chief stopped them:

"Mind your own business. . . . It's a bit closer to the Brazilian side than to ours. . . . Neutral waters . . . And then it's the Ecuadorian flag. I don't even remember what our political relations are with them. . . ."

On the Brazilian side, there were also indifferent watchers.

"It's closer to the Peruvian side," the local police chief there must have said, as he worried about their political relations with Ecuador at the moment.

The ship slowly sank before our eyes along with the remainder of the crew. There is nothing more horrible than people abandoned by others.

I couldn't sleep that night in the village of crocodile hunters, and for some reason recalled Sarapulkin, a bulldozer driver on the Kolyma River. He would not have abandoned them.

Inside the pyramid of Cheops
                    it is oppressive, dank, and eerie.
Rats scurry near the sarcophagus in the dark.
But I will tell you about
                    the sarcophagus of Sarapulkin,
bulldozer driver
            on the Kolyma.
Sarapulkin grew not in height,
                    but in his chest.
It is enormously broad,
                    you could plant oaks on it,
and through his torn rough overalls
a bushy Siberian forest
                    pushes from that chest.
His chest
        and his head are red,
and so is his nose
                and his cheeks and ears!
He could at least share a spare freckle!

83

He is all
          in gold, like a Persian shah.
But he expresses himself,
                    let's be frank, rather crudely.
He pulls back the stick shift
                    and steps on the gas,
looking out from beneath a cap so greasy
you could squeeze it out
                    and fry potatoes!
Rowdy,
          troublemaker,
near the gold-panned murky water
                    of Kolyma,
on his well-earned
                    morning off,
Sarapulkin
          pushes around
                    boulders.
He beeps a warning,
                    a paternal warning,
to the chipmunks
                    peeping out between the roots,
and he forms
          a majestic enigmatic construction,
not a meaningless
                    mound of rocks.
No cemetery,
          with its stupid marble angels,
has anything like it—
                    God damn!
"Listen, Sarapulkin,
                    whatcha piling up here?"
"Comrades,
          I am building my sarcophagus."
"Are you nuts? Lost your marbles?
What's the matter,
                    think you're a pharaoh?"
"Leave me alone,
          you winos,
or help me.

Don't draw flies.
I am
      against historical slavery and serfdom.
I am personally against
                  any cult of personality.
But how,
      I ask you,
                  am I any worse than Cheops?
That's why I'm building myself a sarcophagus.
In Russia,
      comrades,
            pharaoh
was the word the working class
                        used for cops.
All the best things are made
                  by the workers in their millions,
and
   I ask you—
            where are their sarcophagi?
I raised myself a monument
                  with bridges and dams.
Why shove me into the grave,
                  as if into a cellar?
I never
      exploited
            anyone
or let
      myself
            be exploited.
I pity the weak.
            I despise the weak in spirit.
Chiefs get changed,
            fear doesn't change.
I never did time,
            but by nature I am a camp inmate,
because I was forged
                  by the memory of the camps.
Of course, I'm
            no Pushkin or Vysotsky.
It's hard for me to match fame with them,

but I don't like the advice: 'Don't be pushy!'
I want to push up
           to the sky!
Imagine,
      comrades,
             a movie star's horrible life:
all humanity forces itself on her,
                  writes to her,
                      calls up.
I'm cleverer than that.
               I don't need cheap lifetime fame.
I want to be famous after death!
According to the modest,
             that's immodest,
                  impolite,
but I'm building it. . . .
           Let some jerk in the Pentagon
think that a new rocket installation's going up,
but it's Sarapulkin building his sarcophagus!
'What is this thing?'
          a Martian tourist will ask,
walking with his little kids
          in the year 3000,
and he'll be told:
          'Sarapulkin's sarcophagus!
There was this bulldozer driver
          on the Kolyma.'
Well, are you going to help
         or are you off for vodka?
I can tell by your eyes—
         you need a pharaoh.
By the way,
       I use only fuel I've saved,
so it's not costing
       the state anything. . . .
The store's going to close? . . .
         Some hard workers you are!
You're no working class,
      you're just bums!

You'd be better off making your own sarcophagi,
maybe you'd drink less then."
And rejecting all pharaohs outright,
and also winos
                    rushing to the shop,
he sends them all to do
                        something physically impossible—
to go fuck themselves.
That's the Sarapulkin fuku!

The Italian revolutionary Antonio Gramsci once said: "I'm a pessimist
in my observations, but an optimist in my actions."

I saw the ruin of war,
                    but a hypocritical peace is also ruin.
False peacemakers
                    have rats' faces with telltale canary feathers.
To everyone
            who sowed hunger of bodies and souls—
"Fuku!"
We've forgotten the name of the builder of the temple of
                                    Diana of Ephesus,
but we remember who burned it down.
                    Incommensurate honor for a little fascist, a pup.
To all you Herostratuses,
                    castrates,
                            imprisoners,
                                    hangers—
"Fuku!"
Are they worthy of honor,
                    denouncers and toadies?
Why should the names of stoolies
                        ever be spoken?
And yet even Christ is saddled with the sticky name of Judas—
"Fuku!"
For what does that butcher Alexander the Great
                                    deserve statues?

87

Or Napoleon the Pantheon?
                        Why honor that blood-soaked fat man?
All museums are packed with celebrated scoundrels—
"Fuku!"
Like a mustachioed dung beetle,
                              Bismarck crawled into history.
Rasputin is smeared over books
                        like a thick expectoration.
The world encyclopedias are due for a good nose blowing—
"Fuku!"
And for what good deeds
                        haven't you vanished into oblivion,
still flickering on the screen,
                        even though you've turned to dust,
corporal—the Columbus of genocide,
                              blitzkrieg,
                                    and gas chambers?
"Fuku!"
And to you, bloody small-fry,
                        provincial Cheopses,
who crawled over dead bodies
                        just to stay on top,
Somozas and Pinochets,
                  banana generals—
"Fuku!"
To everyone who is elbow deep in blood,
                              but wants to look so clean,
with a supply at the ready
                        of hospitable barbed wire,
to every embryonic ratlet
to every embryonic fascist—
"Fuku!"
Jack Ruby is more famous than Bosch.
But the fame of nonentities
                        is nonexistent,
and if pushing the button ever comes into anyone's fool head,
the planet will wail
                        its last word with a howl:
"Fuku!"

Siqueiros was painting my portrait.

Between us on a paint-splattered stool stood a bottle of wine, from which he and I drank in turn, because we were both pretty exhausted.

The canvas was turned with its back to me, and I could not see what was going on.

Siqueiros had the face of Mephistopheles.

Two hours later, as we had agreed, Siqueiros stuck his brush in the now-empty bottle and abruptly turned the canvas face side to me.

"Well?" he demanded triumphantly.

I said nothing, staring at something squashed, rock-hard, and spiritless.

But what could I say to a man who had fought first against Pancho Villa and then with him, and had later participated in the attempt to assassinate Trotsky?

However, I did mumble shyly:

"I think there's something missing. . . ."

"What?" Siqueiros asked masterfully, as if his chest were once again crisscrossed with bandoliers.

"A heart," I managed to say.

Siqueiros did not lift an eyebrow. His revolutionary experience made itself evident.

"We'll make one," he said in the voice of a man prepared to hold up a bank.

He took the brush out of the bottle, dipped it in bright-red paint, and instantly drew a heart, shaped like an upside-down ace of spades, on my chest.

Then he winked and added an inscription in the corner with the same paint:

One of Yevtushenko's thousand faces. Later I'll do the 999 that are missing. And he dated and signed it.

Trying not to look at the portrait, I changed the subject.

"Aseyev, the poet, once wrote about Mayakovsky: 'There are flimsy stories, swirling the dust on gossip's roads, that in faraway Mexico he left an abandoned child.' You knew Mayakovsky when he was in Mexico. . . . Is it true that he has a son?"

Siqueiros laughed.

"Don't waste your time looking far. . . . Tomorrow morning, when you shave, look in your mirror."

89

It's too early to say my last word—
                              I speak almost at the end,
like a half-vanished ancestor
                              dragging my body between two eras.
I am
  an accidental scrap,
              an apple core of this century
                              which left no leftovers.
History choked on me,
                gnawed on me,
                              but didn't swallow me.
Almost at the end:
I am
    a cracked but exact
                    living death mask of wartime evacuation,
and to be recognized,
                I need no name tag.
In a blizzard I was sculpted
                      by the rusty hands of the Transsiberian—
                          the scraping buffers of train cars.
Almost at the end:
In pants rough as the devil's hide
                          I walked like a son of hell.
Each pant leg thundered in the frost
                          like a frozen drainpipe,
and the "devil's hide" grew on my own
                              and wouldn't pull off,
and in fights saved my backbone,
                        fragile but unbreakable.
Almost at the end:
Once I cried
            in the shadow of spattered, roadside branches,
leaning my head
              on the red and yellow No Thru Way sign,
and everything that they tried to squeeze down my throat,
                          at their gluttonous banquets,
I puked from my guts,
                turning them inside out.
Almost at the end:
History danced on me many times

90

                                    in muddy boots and ballet slippers.
I was not on the stage,
          I was the stage in the blood of my epoch,
                                    in the vomit of this age,
and everything in my life
               which seemed to you not my blood,
                                    but just the thirst for fame,
I do not doubt
               someday you'll call heroic deeds.
Almost at the end:
I am just the ragtag voice of all the voiceless,
                    I am just a faint trace of all the traceless.
I am the half-scattered ashes
                         of somebody's unknown novel.
In your respectable entrance halls
               I am the ambassador of all dead-end streets.
I am a ghost of barracks and plank beds,
               bedbugs,
                    lice,
                         flea markets,
                              and thieves' dens.
Almost at the end:
Half my life
          I searched hopelessly with a bent fork
               for even a hint of meat
                              in canteen cutlets.
Once, when not even ten,
                    I screamed a mother oath
                         in front of my horrified aunt.
I will come to my successors
               as though in Lermontov's epaulets,
police hands on my shoulders,
                    with their polite suggestion:
                              "Let's go buddy!"
Almost at the end:
I am
     the same age to all ages.
I am
     the countryman to all countries
                    even to faraway galaxies.

91

Like an Indian in the rusty handcuffs of Columbus,
                              before my death I shall rasp out:
"Fuku!"
         to those falsely immortal tyrants.
Almost at the end:
A poet today,
              like a coin of Peter the Great,
                              has become really rare.
He even frightens his neighbors on the globe.
But I'll find understanding with my successors
                              one way or another.
Almost candid.
              Almost dying.
                   Almost at the end.

MY UNIVERSITIES

I learned not only from those
                              who brightly beam out of golden frames,
but from everyone whose ID photo
                              didn't come out quite right.
More than from Tolstoy
                    I learned from blind beggars
who sang in train cars about Count Tolstoy.
From barracks
      I learned more than from Pasternak
                              and my verse style was hot "barracko."
I took lessons on Yesenin
                              in snack bars from invalids of war
who tore their striped sailor shirts
                              after spilling out their plain secrets.
Mayakovsky's stepped verse
                         didn't give me as much
as the dirty steps of staircases
                              with handrails polished by kids' pants.
I learned in Zima Junction
                         from my most untalkative Grannies
not to be afraid of cuts, scratches,
                              and various other scrapes.
I learned from dead-end streets that smell of cats,
                              from crooked spattered lanes,
to be sharper than a knife,
                         more ordinary than a cigarette butt.
Empty lots were my shepherds.
                              Waiting lines my nursing mothers.
I learned from all the young toughs
                              who gave me a whipping.
I learned
      from pale-faced harried hacks
with fatal content in their verse
                              and empty content in their pockets.
I learned from all the oddballs in attics,

                    from the dress cutter Alka
who kissed me
                in the dark of a communal kitchen.
I was put together out of the birthmarks of the Motherland
                                from scratches and scars,
cradles and cemeteries,
                    hovels and temples.
My first globe was a rag ball,
                        without foreign threads,
with brick crumbs sticking to it,
and when I forced my way to
                    the real globe,
I saw—it was also made of scraps
                            and also subject to blows.
And I cursed the bloody soccer game,
            where they play with the planet without refs or rules,
and any tiny scrap of the planet,
                    which I touched,
                                I celebrated!
I went round the planet
                    as if it were a gigantic Zima Station,
and I learned from the wrinkles of old women,
                        now Vietnamese, now Peruvian.
I learned folk wisdom
                    taught by the worldwide poor and scum,
the Eskimo's smell for ice,
                    and the Italian's smiling non-despair.
I learned from Harlem
                    not to consider poverty poor,
like a Black
            whose face is only painted white.
And I understood that the majority bends
                            its neck on behalf of others,
and in the wrinkles of those necks
                        the minority hides as if in trenches.
I am branded with the brand of the majority.
                        I want to be their food and shelter.
I am the name of all without names.

I am a writer for all who don't write.
I am a writer
          created by readers,
and readers are created by me.
                    My debt has been paid.
Here I am
          your creator and your creation,
an anthology of you,
                    a second edition of your lives.
I stand more naked than Adam,
                    rejecting court tailors,
the embodiment of imperfections—
                    yours and my own.
I stand on the ruins
          of loves I destroyed.
The ashes of friendships and hopes
                    coldly fly through my fingers.
Choking on muteness
          and the last man to get in line,
I would die for any one of you,
                    because each of you is my homeland.
I am dying from love
          and I howl with pain like a wolf.
If I despise you—
          I despise myself even more.
I could fail without you.
                    Help me to be my real self,
not to stoop to pride,
          not to fall into heaven.
I am a shopping bag stuffed
                    with all the world's shoppers.
I am everybody's photographer,
                    a *paparazzo* of the infamous.
I am your common portrait,
                    where so much remains to be painted.
Your faces are my Louvre,
          my private Prado.
I am like a video player,

95

                          whose cassettes are loaded with you.
I am an attempt at diaries by others
                          and an attempt at a worldwide newspaper.
You have written yourself
                          with my tooth-marked pen.
I don't want to teach you.
                          I want to learn from you.

BEING LATE

Something dangerous
                is beginning:
I am coming late
              to my own self.
I made an appointment
                with my thoughts—
the thoughts
           were snatched
                  from me.
I made an appointment
                with Faulkner—
but they made me
              go to a banquet.
I made an appointment
                with history—
but a grass widow
              dragged me into bed.
Worse
      than barbed wire
are birthday parties,
                mine and others',
and roast suckling pigs
              hold me
like a sprig of parsley
                between their teeth!
Led away for good
to a life absolutely not my own,
everything that I eat,
              eats me,
everything that I drink,
                drinks me.
I made an appointment
                with myself,
but they invite me
              to feast on my own spareribs.
I am garlanded
           from all sides

not by strings of bagels,
                        but by the holes of bagels,
and I look like
                an anthology
                        of zeros.
Life gets broken
                into hundreds of lifelets,
that exhaust
                and execute me.
In order
        to get through to myself
I had to smash my body
                        against others,
and my fragments,
                my smithereens
are trampled
                by the roaring crowd.
I am trying
        to glue myself together,
but my arms
                are still severed.
I'd write
        with my left leg,
but both the left
                and the right
have run off
                in different directions.
I don't know
                where is my body?
And my soul?
Did it really fly off,
without a murmured
                "good-bye!"?
How do I break through
                        to a faraway namesake,
waiting for me
                somewhere in the cold?
I've forgotten
                under which clock

I am waiting
          for myself.
For those who don't know
                    who they are,
time
    does not exist.
No one is
          under the clock.
On the clock
          there is nothing.
I am late for my appointment
                    with me.
There is no one.
               Nothing but cigarette butts.
Only one flicker—
          a lonely,
                    dying
                         spark . . .

WHO ARE YOU, GRAND CANYON?

A thing
     laminating,
          ever bifurcating,
a thing
     melting away
          from itself,
frightened
     by its own terrible weight,
like a lizard
     hiding its soul from the tourists
beneath the rocks.
A thing
     unimaginably old,
something of the very beginning,
          something of the end,
something
     of Cain and Abel.
Womb of the ages,
     turned inside out,
a sphinx
     whose enigma,
          aired out by time,
unsolved by us,
drips away into oblivion.
The body of history,
          not split into chapters,
but ripped asunder by a tomahawk,
both guts and dung.
Granite sandwiches
     of red icebergs,
as if, like sunflower seeds,
          they had pressed into oilcakes
all the blood of the murdered, drop by drop.
Creases,
     like all the wrinkles of mankind
gathered together by eternity. Grand Canyon.

Who are you, Grand Canyon?
                    What is it you want?
You
     are the circles of Dante's hell.
Noah's Ark,
              Babylon.
                    Hellas.
Roman circuses—
                    luxuria of tyrants
on the Arizona sand.
In each of your scorching grains
hide Huns,
              Aztecs,
                    Incas
like fire in tiny pieces of coal.
These precipices
                    are redskin chiefs
lodging their wary thoughts
in the cauldron
                    with spears.
You
     are the partition in all the pyramids,
the walls of the Kremlin
                        with the ghost
of Ivan the Terrible in his cowl.
Who are you, Grand Canyon?
The answer strains.
The rocks struggle.
                    Each one is a clever devil.
They want to press each other down,
but there are no victors:
all are injured
              by the struggle,
all are defeated,
              all are pinned down
by the weight of years.
The rocks languish from the senseless combat.
Afterwards
              they huddle together,

101

and embrace,
and break apart,
hoarsely wheezing at the end.
Those who ruled in grandeur,
all Macedonians,
                    Xerxes and Dariuses,
the planters of fear in souls—
fleas
      who only seemed to be giants—
what have they become today
                              in the Grand Canyon?
Red dust
        in the nostrils of mules.
Wretched,
          like Napoleon in Egypt,
I could almost cry out:
                        "Help me!,"
standing before the face of immortality.
Where is the emperor's cocked hat?
In layers of red,
like a needle in a haystack.
I see—
        jutting out in basalt thickness
the gaunt brush of Hitler's mustache—
hey mule,
          chew it up—it's a trifle!
Into the Grand Canyon
                      with all who are sick
                                            with megalomania!
As a guest in the abyss,
                          the dwarf will quickly understand
that he is a dwarf.
Who are you, Grand Canyon?
                            The stratification
of inexplicable existence—
like volumes upon volumes.
Here is no mountainette
                        from Disney World.
Like the complete works of Dostoyevsky,

102

mountains of suffering,
mountains of wisdom!
Nearby newspapers turned to stone,
but unfortunately,
                    grown no wiser—
mountains of dung.
Who are you, Grand Canyon?
                              You are like the Revolution.
Your roaring waterfalls are uncontrollable,
like the rebellion of Spartacus.
Above the shoals of the Colorado
cliffs—
        like barricades in Paris—
make you young,
                    old man.
You
    sail proudly
above the raging torrents
                        like the battleship *Potyomkin*,
that immortalized a princeling's name.
Sputnik there in shadows,
                          blacker than pitch,
is like the flashlight of Ché Guevara,
somewhere hiding till today.
Who are you, Grand Canyon?
                          The image of America.
There are trails like workers'
                        and farmers' veins—
they almost could elect you President!
The air of Whitman,
                    Robert Frost,
but look around,
                there are chasms beyond chasms.
Hawks in the sky,
                  black ravens,
clans of trees,
                grown out above the abyss,
are the descendants of emigrant
                                families

who have not forgotten their own land.
The wind—
                    a prayerful Mormon chorus.
Cactuses—
                    the unshaven hippies of the incline.
As if they were students,
                              sudden avalanches.
Like the silent majority,
                    the cliffs
have a hard icy crust
                    on their foreheads.
You were made, Grand Canyon,
                              not by the rules.
You are a skyscraper
                    only turned inward.
A stone apple pie.
You,
      Grand Canyon,
                    are filled with chimeras,
like a Notre Dame de Paris of America,
and are cluttered with things,
                              like a barn.
You,
      like America,
                    are restless and not in place,
you
    like her,
            are uncoordinated and dissonant.
But even though split asunder,
                    you are whole—
that's how God made you,
                    with a Frank Lloyd Wright
devil's daring.
Who are you, Grand Canyon?
                              You are the people's reward.
A young girl descends to the Colorado River.
About sixteen.
            She is so delighted,
sleeping gear juts out of her rucksack.

She looks about unearthly,
                         heavenly.
A dog on a safety leash
pulls her
          along the edge of the abyss.
This tourist is a little different:
she has no fear of the deadly risk,
she has no desire to cling to the shadows.
She moves strangely,
                         stepping cautiously.
Shudder, Grand Canyon:
                         SHE IS BLIND.
Let not a tiny stone strike her.
Quietly she moves on the leash above the river,
touching the sky with her free hand,
caressing tenderly the clouds with her cheeks
in the morning hour.
There is something of an old woman in her step,
but on her face so many freckles—
childlike, all-seeing eyes!
Greedily gulping the air
her skin sees
              the Grand Canyon,
the miracle of its beauty.
And wounded by its healing beauty,
a blind girl
              down in the Grand Canyon
is,
   Grand Canyon,
                above you.

"A SMALL DISH . . ."

A small dish darkens in the shadows,
dribbled with wax that did not burn. . . .
A candle, melted on the table,
will not return.

Deft technicians can plane verse
into curls and fancy turns,
but the charm of Pushkin's curls
will not return.

After so many lips, like a bitter trace,
remains the taste of a poisoned urn,
but the taste of watermelon in childhood
will not return.

He who breaks up a family,
another one will never earn,
and friendship trampled underfoot
will not return.

On leashes in alien hands
great nations each other spurn,
and people—even from the heavens—
will not return.

On fat mugs with honeyed lips
bloodstained traces we discern.
A face once turned into a fat mug
will not return.

Only with the revolt of shame
against shamelessness
will we escape the Day of Judgment—
honestly, more or less.

Only with the revolt of the face
against facelessness

will life return again
in all its divine mess.

Shamelessness can devour children—
and never cease to yearn.
But shame is not frightening. Shame is not death.
Everything will return.

YOU STILL HAVEN'T RETURNED

You still haven't returned
all my letters
        and haven't thrown them out in the trash,
but you distance yourself,
as if the block of ice, where we live—
                were cut in two.
You sleep most innocently,
as if you were beside me—
          only an arm's length away,
but this fissure
grinds the deathlike starch of the sheet.
You distance yourself,
and it is terrible, that it's done bit by bit,
               without haste.
You shut yourself off
from me as though
        from a still-not-dead
            soul.
You take away everything—
both so many shared years
         and our two children.
You are pulling away
like living skin
       from my living bones.
The pain of estrangement
cuts carelessly,
      brutalizes.
           On our ribs there's blood and slime
along the fracture line
of two souls,
      which had almost grown together.
Oh, that double-damned
almost-impossible-to-overcome "almost"!
How can
     everything crucified

or almost already crucified
                          be saved?
Easily,
      skillfully,
like piranhas, leaving only a skeleton on the bottom,
petty little things devoured
still one more unrelivable love.
But devouring
is contagious,
                 like the black plague,
and love that's been betrayed
                              turns to treason on its own.
And some howling thing
clutches at the children,
                          without hiding its claws in fur.
Love is a monster
that devours even its own children.
For the time I spent pub crawling,
for devouring the best years of life,
I beg with most Christian humility—
forgive me,
            don't devour me in revenge.
There is a trite expression:
a woman has, as they say, no past.
I am
    your past,
and, that means, there's no me.
                          I am my own skeleton.
I carry in horror
my remains to the hostile bed.
For the nonexistent
it's no easier to exist.
My beloved,
resurrect me,
              your own child,
mold me,
        mold me
from all the remains,

from yourself,
        from nothing.
You are
     my future,
my momentary and eternal star.
Perhaps loving,
but forgetting how one loves . . .
         forever?

DON'T DISAPPEAR

Don't disappear. . . . By disappearing from me,
you will disappear from yourself,
betraying your own self forever,
and that will be the basest dishonesty.

Don't disappear. . . . To disappear is so easy.
It's impossible to resurrect one another.
Death drags down too deep.
Death even for a moment is too long.

Don't disappear. . . . Forget the third shadow.
In love there are only two. There are no thirds.
We both will be pure on Judgment Day,
when the trumpets call us to account.

Don't disappear. . . . We have redeemed sin.
We both are free of the law, we are sinless.
We are worthy together of the forgiveness of those
whom we have unintentionally wounded.

Don't disappear. . . . One can disappear in an instant,
but how could we meet later in the centuries ahead?
Is your double possible in the world,
and my double? Only barely in our children.

Don't disappear. . . . Give me your palm.
I am written on it—this I believe.
What makes one's last love terrible
is that it is not love, but fear of loss.

UNDER THE SKIN OF THE STATUE OF LIBERTY

(An Excerpt)

Senator Robert Kennedy had unusual eyes.

They were always tense.

Like pale-blue razor blades they pierced through anyone in conversation with him as if someone dangerous were lurking behind the person's back.

Even when the Senator smiled and his golden forelock leaped on a mountain skier's peeling, sunburned forehead, and blinding white teeth capered in his mouth like children on the grass, his eyes lived a separate, guarded life. For his birthday today he wore a bright green jacket, raspberry bowtie, gay plaid trousers and light suede shoes. However, all of this bright, multicolored clothing was planned to distract the guests from the main thing—the host's eyes.

The Senator's energetic hands assisted his guests in removing their overcoats and tousled the clipped heads of numerous little Kennedys who had composed some domestic jazz and were rapturously banging on metal plates. The Senator's thin lips smile, knowing full well how enchantingly they do it, and at the same time they manage to say something particularly pleasant to each guest.

But the Senator's eyes—two blue clots of will and anxiety—caressed no one on the head, smiled at no one. They inhabited his face like two beings uninvolved in the general gaiety. Within these eyes an exhausting hidden work transpired.

"Remember my words—this man will be President of the United States," Averell Harrimann said, bending toward me.

The table was dominated by the celebrated columnist Art Buchwald, who looked like a kindhearted, well-fed tomcat that nonetheless from time to time loved to dig his claws into those who petted him.

Buchwald artfully demonstrated his independence by deftly and casually ridiculing everything and everybody, including the master of the house. Wise kings always invited mercilessly venomous jesters to their festivities. Jesters have always ridiculed kings in their presence, which made them appear even wiser. A tamed accuser is not frightening, but rather useful. However, only wise kings have understood this.

And Robert Kennedy, laughing loudly in delight at Buchwald's talented mockery of him, embraced the columnist, and they clinked their glasses together.

But the Senator's eyes continued to work.

Meanwhile, a game of blindman's buff was organized.

A long-legged artist, who had put a black band over her eyes, wandered about the room in uncertainty, her arms, draped in red chiffon, stretched out searchingly.

Her fingers, manicured the color of the moon, were barely stirring as they approached the tongue of flame flickering above a candle.

"Watch out, you'll burn yourself on the candle . . ." said the Senator, standing nearby.

"And that's you, Bobby." The woman burst out laughing and rushed in the direction of his voice.

Bobby adroitly dodged her and leaped away toward a wall. But the woman with the black band over her eyes went straight toward him, preventing an escape route with her outstretched arms.

Bobby pressed himself against the wall as though he were trying to squeeze himself into it, but the wall would not let him in.

When the evening had reached its end, Robert Kennedy and I stood alone in the corridor. In our hands were antique crystal goblets in which tiny green sparks of champagne were dancing.

"Tell me, do you really want to become President?" I asked. "It seems to me that it's a rather thankless job."

"I know," he grinned. Then he became serious. "But I would like to continue my brother's work."

"Then, let's drink to that," I said. "But in order for it to come true, according to an old Russian custom, we must drink the goblets right to the bottom and then smash them against the floor. . . ."

Glancing at the goblets, Robert Kennedy suddenly became embarrassed.

"All right, only I must ask Ethel's permission. These are heirlooms from her dowry. . . ."

He disappeared with the crystal goblets and appeared later, still more embarrassed: "Wives will be wives . . . I got some other glasses that were on hand in the kitchen. . . ."

It surprised me somewhat that one could think about some insignificant glasses when such a toast was being proposed, but of course, wives will be wives. We drank in one gulp and simultaneously threw down the emptied goblets. But they didn't break and, bouncing softly, rolled over the red shag of the rug.

I have always been superstitious and a terrible foreboding passed through me. I looked at Robert Kennedy. He had turned pale. Probably he too was superstitious. In this respect politicians aren't very different from poets.

The work in the Senator's eyes came to a halt. They grew still, staring at the unbroken goblets.

Robert Kennedy picked up one of them and tapped it with his finger. The sound was muted and dull.

The goblets were made of transparent plastic.

Since then I never ask others to break their glasses, nor do I try myself.

"I, Robert Kennedy, Bobby,
                    was shot by the age,
nominated to the gods
                    in the absence of a god.
Money was good to me.
                    People loved me
for my name—or
                    for my blue eyes.
But there is a special something
                    on the brow of the favored,
like the cross of murder
                    on the doors of the Huguenots.
And I was slain,
                    not as an example to hypocrites—
but because a forelock too eagerly
                    distinguished itself against the gray.
It's easy to aim at a lamp.
                    It's difficult at something not concrete.
Brightness is talent's weakness.
                    Grayness the strength of the ungifted.
With a vengeance I have hated
                    grayness—the curse of the age—
from the time when, at my brother's side,
                    I became the Attorney General.
With no satisfaction
                    and a heavy heart,

114

I climbed into skyscrapers of denunciations.
                              Their architect is grayness!
Grayness chokes zealously,
                    grayness chokes duplicity,
all attempts not to be
                    gray, at least in part.
Grayness is a whore, an ignoramus,
                              but passions are not alien to her.
Grayness leaped from calumny as though from a trampoline
                              and is in power!
Like a millrace for washing ore
                    grayness sifts through souls.
Whole nuggets are coming down from the ravine!
                              Our gold is grayness!
Throughout the land
                    talent is put into storage
like merchandise that has lost its value.
                    The demand is for grayness, for grayness!
You who inhabit this place, look around you
                              at how freely sprawled
and growing into the seat
                    is the grayness with the chairlike behind.
You who inhabit this place, don't listen
                    to the persuasion of the swamp:
'After all, gray is better
                    than something bloody . . .'
You ought to tremble with a ghastly shudder
                              at a cozy dinner—
for the brown horror
                    is shoving its way behind the grayness.
Instead of idylls, you ought to remember,
                              when slicing your pudding,
how they sank into my forelock
                    a clot of grayness—a bullet . . ."

COME TO MY MERRY GRAVE

Come to my graveside,
come sober or drunk.
Both sandals and boots
I'll hear above me.

Bring pine and rowan branches
or any that you wish,
bring the ones you love,
bring along the kids.

Sit down on the grass and bench,
open some wine if it's there,
don't be embarrassed before me—
render the dead its due.

Speak of the pain that is hidden
which tortures you from below,
speak, if only of football—
I fear losing touch with the crowd.

Neither granite nor colored marble,
exalted tears or speeches brave,
but just make more sweet nonsense
over my merry grave.

Give honor to what's not been quoted!
Forget the author of books.
Recall the liar, the friend. Let out
a kindergarten-cannibal shout.

Cook up lies and tales about me,
but keep the fibs
of Siberia and Tahiti
a little like my own.

For in my boastful, willful life
between the hawks and doves,

one bit was really true—
that is, I really was.

Fables turn out to be true
and facts wound round with legend,
but scandal didn't kill me
and legend cannot do it now.

I will remain not only by my verse,
my golden charm is this:
I loved unmeasured this whole earth
and she fell in love with me.

And the earth wanted me,
so that people could not tell
where is my end-of-summer body,
where earth's fun-loving last.

It's sweet with bone-chilled edge
to understand, when all is done,
that I'll seep through rainy slipperiness
between the toes of barefoot urchins.

I don't have the strength to die completely.
Obituaries and mourning are a bunch of rot.
Only come to my graveside,
to the grave where I am not.

MOMMA AND THE NEUTRON BOMB

(An Excerpt)

Momma,
       I've been reading today's newspapers
through the transparent-with-hunger children of Leningrad
who have come to the global Christmas tree for murdered children.
Tiny shriveled hands from Piskaryovskoye Cemetery
reach out for the yellow lanterns
                        of tree decoration tangerines,
but when they pluck them
               they don't know what to do with them.
Children of Auschwitz,
               with convulsed, little blue faces,
choking on gas,
          ask Santa Claus for the gift
of a glass bauble from the tree,
               inside of which
there's just a tiny bit of oxygen.
Unborn babies from My Lai,
               ripped from their mothers' wombs,
crawl
     to a sobbing Big Bad Wolf.
Little Red Riding Hood
             struggles to glue together pieces
of children blown up by bombs
             in Belfast and Beirut.
Children of El Salvador,
             who had been frightened by a vindictive tank,
recoil in horror
         from a toy one.
The dancing circle of murdered children
            round their global Christmas tree is endless.
But if a neutron bomb goes off
            there will be no children at all:
there will only be kindergartens
          where teddy bears will howl

as they tear with plastic claws
                         their chests of plush right to the sawdust inside,
and inflated elephants
                         will trumpet a belated alarm. . . .
Thank you, Samuel Cohen
                         and other humanitarians,
for your new "toy"—
not one for children to play with,
but one that plays with children,
until there isn't a single child left—
for the disappearance of the line in "Children's World" store,
for the end of the shortage of paper diapers,
for Disneyland,
              where now
                         no one
                              will break anything,
for the dolls
              whose pigtails will never be cruelly pulled off,
for the windows
              that will never be broken by rude footballs,
for the forever riderless
                         merry-go-round ponies,
creaking in the worldwide emptiness,
for children's tights,
carefully hung out on wash lines,
                              which never will be torn
in a game of hide-and-seek amidst the brambles. . . .
A final worldwide hide-and-seek game will take place.
There will be no children.
                         There will be no adults.
Safe and sound streets
                         will be strewn with safe and sound wristwatches
with fastened straps and bands
still retaining the shape of vanished wrists,
with wedding rings fallen from fingers,
with turquoise and other earrings
                              fallen from women's lobes,
and only safe and sound empty gloves

        will grip
safe and sound steering wheels of safe and sound cars.
The whole international display of women's legs in Perugia
will vaporize:
      only empty shoes will remain
with a handful of ash imprinted in gold on the insoles,
and between the suede and patent leather urns
a half-fused small chain
        from the ankle
of a vaporized Peruvian girl
        will crawl and sniff about the heels.
There will be no Momma either.
        Only her newsstand will remain,
on which an atomic wind will leaf through
moldy editions that have become antiques:
Football and Hockey,
      America, and *Health.*
And the ghost of Momma's butcher
        turned into vapor
will by habit leave
      for Momma's ghost
the ghost of a frozen chicken—
        a fellow countryman of Maupassant
from a country
      where safe and sound Maupassant is on the bookshelves
and not a single fellow countryman is safe and sound.
And a new Major Firby,
       after pressing a Hiroshima button,
will see how Europe is turned into
        a dead Euroshima,
and the major won't be able to go crazy,
       since he'll have become a ghost himself.
Momma rarely talks about politics,
but this is what she once said
on return from a wallpaper store
on Star Boulevard
where her buttons were torn off by accident
in the scramble for wallpaper from East Germany:

"My God,
          what people won't do out of greed for things.
That's probably why
               they invented the neutron bomb. . . ."
And I imagined
          millions of stores all over the world
packed with wallpaper,
               mink coats,
diamonds,
          Italian shoes,
Japanese stereos,
          cans of Danish beer,
where there will be everything,
                    but the one thing that's disappeared—
a customer.
Pillows will start looting
               Neanderthal skulls from museums.
Shirts
     all alone
          will pull themselves on statues and skeletons.
Children's strollers will rock
               babies bottled in alcohol from medical labs.
Razor blades
          will want to slit their own throats
                         from loneliness.
There will be a mass hanging of neckties from trees.
Books, longing for eyes and fingers,
                    will organize self-immolations.
Things, it is possible, will adapt themselves.
               By themselves things will start going to stores
and, very likely, will create universal havoc
when an unverified rumor circulates
that in some store in the suburbs
                    a man had suddenly appeared on sale.
Things are bound to come to political blows
and, probably, some eager-beaver refrigerator
will devise a new neutron bomb,
which destroys

        only things
and leaves people
           safe and sound. . . .
But what will remain
            if people don't remain?
He who takes up the atomic sword
             will perish by the same!

DISBELIEF IN YOURSELF IS INDISPENSABLE

While you're alive it's shameful to worm your way into
                                  the Calendar of Saints.
Disbelief in yourself is more saintly.
It takes real talent not to dread being terrified
by your own agonizing lack of talent.

Disbelief in yourself is indispensable.
Indispensable to us is the loneliness
                                  of being gripped in the vise,
so that in the darkest night the sky will enter you
and skin your temples with the stars,
so that streetcars will crash into the room,
wheels cutting across your face,
so the dangling rope, terrible and alive,
will float into the room and dance invitingly in the air.

Indispensable is any mangy ghost
in tattered, overplayed stage rags,
and if even the ghosts are capricious,
I swear, they are no more capricious than those who are alive.

Indispensable amidst babbling boredom
are the deadly fear of uttering the right words
and the fear of shaving, because across your cheekbone
graveyard grass already grows.

It is indispensable to be sleeplessly delirious,
to fail, to leap into emptiness.
Probably, only in despair is it possible
to speak all the truth to this age.

It is indispensable, after throwing out dirty drafts,
to explode yourself and crawl before ridicule,
to reassemble your shattered hands
from fingers that rolled under the dresser.

Indispensable is the cowardice to be cruel
and the observation of the small mercies,
when a step toward falsely high goals
makes the trampled stars squeal out.

It's indispensable, with a misfit's hunger,
to gnaw a verb right down to the bone.
Only one who is by nature from the naked poor
is neither naked nor poor before fastidious eternity.

And if from out of the dirt,
                              you have become a prince,
                                             but without principles,
unprince yourself and consider
how much less dirt there was before,
when you were in the real, pure dirt.
Our self-esteem is such baseness. . . .
The Creator raises to the heights
only those who, even with tiny movements,
tremble with the fear of uncertainty.

Better to cut open your veins with a can opener,
to lie like a wino on a spit-spattered bench in the park,
than to come to that very comfortable belief
in your own special significance.

Blessed is the madcap artist,
who smashes his sculpture with relish—
hungry and cold—but free
from degrading belief in himself.

THE UNEXPRESSED

The unexpressed,
                    the unarticulated
are frightening,
                    when as fragments
they burn
            beneath the skin,
with no way at all
                    to be scratched out,
plucked out,
            or brought to reason.
Events
        bricked up inside
cry out in despair:
                    "We've been forgotten.
We'll be eliminated
                    from history.
Let us out!
            Let us out!"
Suffering rises up
                    like a lump in the throat:
"We are
        like stifled sobs.
We long so
            for our liberation:
Express us!
            Express us!"
Smashing through ribs,
                        new ideas call out their appeal:
"We are crowded inside.
                    We are torn to pieces there."
Words that are beautiful,
                        but unuttered
scream:
        "We have been buried alive."
And all mistakes,
                sins that have been secreted,

pound themselves
                    like epileptics, saying:
"That which is not expressed
                         will be forgotten,
and what is forgotten
                    will happen again."
Repentance gnaws out:
                         "I need to break loose.
I was a tiny thing.
                    Now I am full grown!"
Grief,
        not expressed in time,
howls in twilight:
                    "I want to be free!"
And joy weeps
            quite joylessly.
And gentleness whispers: "Why,
                            tormenting one another,
                                do you conceal,
not only the worst
                but even the best?
Hidden pain
            is terrifying
and inevitably
            will kill,
but even gentleness is deadly,
                            if
it is concealed. . . ."
Start the confession,
                    even slowly, bit by bit.
Make an attempt
                to begin,
                        to try.
When a confession
                is whole and done,
then what prevails
                is admonition.
But we are shy,
                like wrongful accusations,
not only of what is terrible,

                              but even of what is beautiful.
We are shy about love,
                    acting as if we were too young,
and conceal even
                love of country.
But I don't believe
                in that kind of sincerity:
there is in it something obviously
                                unsubstantiated—
when the simplest cowardice
                          to speak out
plays
      at subtle understatement.

DIRECTNESS

There is a directness
                that's like something crooked.
It is hunchbacked inside itself.
Before it,
      life is guiltlessly guilty
for not being a simple drawing.
Be afraid of making life straight,
                   without understanding
that by straightening you can bend.
Sometimes in history the straight line
between two points
             is the longest route.

COMRADES BUTWHATIFERS

Not every idea sprouts,
                not every seed breaks through the asphalt.
With his fist Archimedes
                pounded the globe like the All Mighty:
"Give me the right fulcrum
                and I will lift the whole earth,"
but they didn't give it to him, saying:
                "But what if . . ."
"But what if . . ."
                they had put sticks through the wheels
of the first locomotive—
                pushing it off the track,
and blacksmiths had grabbed
                the scalpel of the surgeon,
who for the first time
                opened a heart to save it.
"But what if . . ."
                some sated smug mugs
had grumbled against flying machines
                and Edison's lamp.
"But what if . . ."
                banned by their fears,
Bulgakov's *Master and Margarita*
                was published later by twenty years.
Saying good-bye to rotgut
                is torture for an alcoholic.
Pretzels forgotten by drinkers
                sadly drown in borsch.
But there are alcoholics of cowardice—
                a special breed apart.
They are "Comrades Butwhatifers,"
                a juicy new word.
Their hands tremble,
                as though they had the d.t.'s
when asked to sign their names
                to poems, plans, and designs,

and even water pitchers
                          bubble alcoholically
in the hands of alcoholics of cowardice,
                                    the rotgutters of lies.
And inside telephone wires,
                          crawling from ear to ear,
as through oversweetened tubing,
                                comes the verbal rotgut.
Instead of worries about wheat
or meat
        or steel,
we hear a sticky mumbling:
"But . . . what . . . if . . . but . . . what . . . if . . ."
The Russian doubting Thomas,
copulating with the telephone,
like a society samovar
in the Russian Tea Room,
boils with civic doubts.
His copper forehead comes unsoldered.
A stream of steam spurts through the seam.
But it's all for him ridiculously simple:
"But . . . what . . . if . . . but . . . what . . . if . . ."
It's high time to exhibit Filonov
so that even Paris might swoon.
But for them this great name smells
                                like a lit fuse:
"But . . . what . . . if . . ."
While great truths are seeking proof,
our days, our years
disappear into nowhere,
sucked out by quiet vampires,
by comrades butwhatifers . . .
How much has been burned out,
                          as in a great drought,
                                by this butwhatiferism.
It's shameful to try to catch
                          belated rain with a sieve!
There are those who gave all their life
                                to create something,

130

and there are drones whose sole labor
                                    is to create nothing.
Their look is aimed
                    like a double-barreled shotgun,
as though a trembling petitioner
                            were a hungry timber wolf.
That safe, crammed with so many undecided fates,
                                        is a coffin of red tape
whose steel-trap teeth
                    wolfishly crunch human souls.
Knights of procrastination,
                        in the armor of resolutions,
masters
        of circular files,
where even long-nosed Nessy
                            could never find the bottom,
are no better than Colorado beetles,
                                like hoof-and-mouth disease,
they ravage wheat and cattle
                            as well as innocent farmers.
Our Mother Earth is widowed,
                            deprived of loving hands that plant,
stalks of buckwheat languish,
                            and clover sags in sadness,
and tormented sheaves of wheat
                            are cut down at the roots
by a falsely great
                State biology,
and in order to dodge pitiless taxes
                        poor chickens have learned to croak like frogs.
In his button-bursting tunic
                        Comrade Butwhatiferinsky,
to protect his dear fellow citizens
                            from so-called harmful tricks,
saw in all of cybernetics
                        only obscurantism and mysticism
and robbed computers
                    from our future children.
And denying everything that's new,

131

                    the procrastinators,
                                the shoverouters
menacingly wave their rubber stamps:
                                "But there is no precedent,"
forgetting that,
            with granddad's old rifle,
                            in lice,
                                    barefoot,
                                        in rags,
the October Revolution also had no precedent!
I look forward to the time
                    when, by the laws of ballistic science,
our dear "comrades butwhatifers,"
                who in place of ideology
                            use only armchairology,
will be catapulted head over heels
                        out of their cozy armchairs.
O great land of ours,
                throw them out
                        from their headless headquarters.
Let them at long last breathe the fresh air
                            of our enormous expanse.
When censuring pencils
            are in the cowardly hands of "comrades butwhatifers,"
there is an enormous chasm
                    between a red banner
                                and a red pencil.
On this banner is embroidered
                    only a hammer and sickle
and not somebody's craven:
                "But . . . what . . . if . . ."

REQUIEM FOR *CHALLENGER*

This white tragic swan
                of farewell explosion,
this white swan of death
                    made from the last breath
                    of seven evaporated souls,
shook the gravestones of Arlington,
                the Kremlin stars,
                    and the ancient armless statues of Rome.
The already gray
           Pyrenees,
           Caucasus,
           and Everest
now are become forever more gray.
Gagarin's brotherly shadow
                shuddered,
immortally crucified on the stars,
and his widow
           began to walk over the ocean
           to her American sister-widows.
The Statue of Liberty,
                crying the green tears of a mermaid,
tried to reach the cosmos
             to save her children,
             but could not.
Our life is a challenge.
                Our planet is our common *Challenger*.
We humiliate her,
           frightening each other with bombs.
But could we explode her?
                Even by mistake?
                Even by accident?
That would be the final error
                never to be undone.

ALDAN GIRL

Aldan girl, well-done girl,
Look at me, who am I?
A guest? A thief from the wildest west,
So ragged is my vest?
I just try to do my best.

In her hand, a hunter's gun.
Watch your step, you hooligan!
She checked me out—I am a guest.
Yet in her eyes, still one request.

She scraped the moss with her boots
As she was trying to find my roots.
She's as graceful as a sable.
Not to love her, I'm quite unable.

From woodcock feathers she'd made a fan.
Come my lovely we'll have some fun.
Señorita from Siberia
Sitting softly on the porch,
Brushing off those courting mosquitoes,
Tasting blood as though hot borsch.

And her mosquito net mantilla
Trembles cautiously on guard.
Though I am silent and boyish,
An old Siberian bard.

I construct with clumsy fingers
A hand-rolled butt from last year's "News."
I joke with words, though I am trying
To share with her my wordless views:

"I've almost reached the end, my dear.
All addresses I forgot.

I've returned to the shadow of your tear
From Buenos Aires, oh my God!

One, who's burned two family houses
Is happy now in just a tent.
My third's inflamed in tears and collapsing.
To save it now, I don't attempt.

I'm not one of those tit-grabbers,
Not one of those liars, but
Don't open your door which squeaks so softly,
Else I'll burn out your blameless hut.

Who am I, what kind of creature?
A full disaster looking for cuddles?
I didn't fall from a pink cloud.
I am out of pits and puddles.

I am a walking, fallen tree. I tease
The other lying fallen trees.
I'm tasty to some men's wives
And to some men's friendly knives.

I'm from those special hoboes,
I'm hoboing inside myself,
In my own birdcage encaged.
And my guts are my bed shelf.
So many sucking swamps inside me.
So many uncuttable jungles.
But something blue and defenseless
flowers, whispers, bangles.

All my life—such a mess, my honey.
All I've done—a false kind of bliss.
But I'm made from forget-me-nots.
I can't forget a single kiss!

Please believe me, the crier-liar,
I destroyed everything—it is done.

But I've never unloved anybody.
I will never unlove anyone.

Even wild flowers are dying,
I am wild, but to die is not clever.
Love is not only love, it's something.
Love is also unloving never!

You are so beautiful now,
Aldan girl, well-done girl, in your blue.
Like a Queen's train behind you gliding,
The mosquitoes with pleasure taste you.
I am a little bit old for you, sweetie.
I'll not find any grace in disgrace.
But allow me just to stand a moment
As close as possible to your face."

MY PERUVIAN GIRL

In the hour when newspapers die,
they change into the rubbish of night,
and a dog with the remains of a biscuit
grows still as he holds me in his sight;

in the hour when instincts are resurrected,
the ones that sanctimoniously hide by day,
taxi drivers cry: "Hey, Gringo!
Una chica Peruana—lez go, oke!";

in the hour when the post office is closed,
and the telegraph chatters sleeplessly,
and a muchacho, wrapped in a poncho,
slumbers, pressed against someone's statue;

in the hour when prostitutes and muses
smear their faces with makeup
and the next day's rubbish is being prepared
in huge-type headlines across the top;

in the hour when everything is unseen and seen,
neither going to nor coming from an invitation,
I wander through the Avenida de Lima
as though it were a cemetery of news.

Covered with spittle and grapefruit rinds,
the street smells like a sewer,
but look over there—a human contour
appears through a pile of newspaper.

This old woman, contorted in deafness,
blaming no one for anything,
has made herself a poncho
from the events of yesterday.

She has wrapped herself up to the eyebrows,
right and left, to hide from the cold.

137

It doesn't matter to her what's left and what's right,
if she could only get a tiny bit warmer.

She is wrapped in scandals, intrigues
and football games—down to her heels.
From under a model's legs
her own bare feet stick out.

Limousines, submarines, rockets
stick to the asphalt when dumped.
Horse races, yachts, striptease and banquets
lay always on her peasant shoulders.

And a white store-window llama
in sorrow sees from behind the glass
the still-warm blood of Vietnam showing
through a photo on her shoulderblades.

From beneath the litter of the world's marketplace,
not knowing how to understand any of it,
like a hunted llama, the Inca woman stares—
humanity's Mother of Sorrows.

The era's injustice has bent her,
whole stories weigh her down,
and, like a living sculpture, she is
the truth of the world beneath a pile of lies.

Oh, you store-window white llama,
nestle up to her hollow chest,
set her free from the rubbish,
lead her away to the Sierra Blanca!

A representative of a Great Power,
I bow to her like a son without words,
before this tormented face—
a face of sorrows with canyons of wrinkles.

Barely breathing beneath the rags,
the greatest power in the world

has crazily taken refuge inside,
you know, it's the human soul.

"Una chica Peruana, Gringo!" they cry
with a hiss, but I remain silent.
I don't want to explain to the taxi drivers
that I have found my Peruvian girl.

SATCHMO

Great Satchmo plays all bathed in sweat.
A salty Niagara pours from his brow,
but when the trumpet rises to the clouds,
it growls,
   it roars.
He played to the whole world
      the way he loved.
He is stolen from us now by the grave,
but even before his birth
he was stolen
   from his sweet Africa.
In secret revenge for the chains of his ancestors
he enslaves us all
    like helpless children.
The whites of his great eyes flicker in sorrow
as he howls and horns about the globe—
this kid from an orphanage
in the town of New Orleans.
Great Satchmo plays all bathed in sweat,
his nostrils smoke
     like two black muzzles,
and teeth dazzle in his mouth
like thirty white projectors.
And the sparkling sweat pours off
as if a beautiful mighty hippo
rose
  snorting,
    from an African river.
Stamping on fan notes with his heel,
and wiping the downpour from his brow,
he throws handkerchief after handkerchief
into the piano's open womb.
Again back to the microphone he goes,
pressing the stage till it cracks,
and each wet handkerchief is as heavy
as the crown of art.

Art is far removed
from the lady whose name is Pose,
and when it labors
it's not ashamed of sweat.
Art is
        not the charm of prattlers,
but, full of movement of heavy things,
the tragic labor of a trumpet player
whose music is tatters of lung.
Though art is bartered and sold,
that's not what it's all about.
The poet
        and the great jazzman
are like brothers
                in their rasping delivery.
Great Satchmo, did you make it to heaven?
We'll never know.
                        But if you're there—play!
Let the good times roll once more!
Shake up
        those boring angels.
But so there'll be no remorse in hell,
so death will cheer us sinners up,
Archangel Gabriel,
pass your horn
                to the better player—
to Louis!

"WHEN THE CLOVER FIELD STIRS . . ."

When the clover field stirs,
when pine trees creak and sigh,
my heart freezes, listens, remembers
that soon someday I will die.

On the roof by the rainspout cool,
a boy will stand up with a plump dove,
and I'll grasp that dying is cruel
to one's self, and to others we love.

No feeling of life without a feeling of death.
We depart, not like water into sand so clever.
But the living, those who relieve the dead,
never take the place of the dead, ever.

Something of this I grasped in life—
that means, I wasn't knocked about for naught.
I forgot, it seems, everything I remembered,
but I remembered everything I forgot.

I understood that snow is fluffier in childhood,
that the hills are greener in youth,
that in life there are so many lives, I understood,
and how many times we love in truth.

I understood that I was secretly connected
at once to so many people from all time.
I understood that man is unhappy because
he is searching for that happiness sublime.

In happiness there are such stupid lies.
Happiness just stares emptily, and easily will sleep.
Misery stares, sadly lowering its eyes,
because it sees so clearly, so deep.

Happiness is like a glimpse from an airplane.
Misery sees the earth without adornments.

In happiness there is something treacherous—
misery never betrays man's laments.

I was imprudently lucky,
thank God—happiness didn't happen.
I wanted that which is impossible.
It's good that I didn't succeed.

I love you, human people,
and I forgive the striving for happiness.
I have now become happy forever,
because I don't search for that mess.

I need only to keep safe the sweetness
of clover on hardened lips so small.
I need only a little weakness—
after all, not to die at all.

A HALF BLADE OF GRASS

Death is still far off
                    and everything is so hard,
as if the way up is on rotted stairs.
Life is getting bitter,
                    like overheated milk
with foam burned black.
They say to me, sighing:
                    "Feel sorry for yourself,"
but I'll take a half blade of grass in my teeth
and already I'm more cheerful
                    from this gift of the field—
from the sourness
            and from the bitterness.
I'll take a gentle bit
                in summer or in spring,
and I am made happy by this green trifle,
and my people
            must have taken pity on me in advance,
because they don't spoil me with pity.
If they smash my ribs smartly in a fight,
I consider
        that's how it's supposed to be.
They jab me in the back
                and don't understand
why I'm not smiling.
In those who were pitied in childhood
there is no strength,
                but pervasive weakness.
A half blade of grass in the teeth—
                        there's my whole secret,
and in the earth to keep growing—
                    there's a half blade of grass.

MURDER

No one sleeps more beautifully than you.
But I am afraid
            that you will waken just now,
and touch me with an indifferent glance, lightly passing,
and commit the murder of beauty.

"WHEN I DEPART . . ."

When I depart forever
                    into never
you'll still be young
                    and fortunately not clever.
I'll do your
            growing old instead
in my eternal ghetto,
                    dark and dead,
but I won't leave you there,
                              to kill, to sever. . . .
You'll still be young,
                    and fortunately not clever.

Yevgeny Yevtushenko, a world-class poet translated into all major languages, is in the forefront of change in Gorbachev's Russia. When "Fuku" was published in *Novy Mir* in September of 1985, it signaled a new openness in Soviet literary circles. Because the work contains numerous passages on many forbidden subjects, including the resurgence of neo-Stalinism and anti-Semitism in the Soviet Union, "Fuku" had to be read and approved for publication by Mikhail Gorbachev himself. Its publication is being recognized as a milestone in contemporary Russian literature and in the long battle over Soviet censorship.